THE WRITING REPERTOIRE

Developing Writing at Key Stage 2

Compiled and edited by
Felicity Ross

Published in September 1996
by the National Foundation for Educational Research,
The Mere, Upton Park, Slough, Berkshire SL1 2DQ

Compiled and edited by:

Felicity Rees
Senior Research Officer, NFER

List of contributors:

Diana M Bentley, Education Consultant

Pam Czerniewska, Former Director, National Writing Project

Julie Daw, Teacher/Education Consultant

Carola Garvie, Section Head, Hertfordshire Assessment Team

Jane Girle, Deputy Headteacher, Cookham Rise Primary School

Sylvia Karavis, Advisory Teacher, PAGE, Oxfordshire

Gaynor Kitchener, Associate Adviser (English), Cheshire

Jenny Monk, Senior Lecturer, Westminster College, Oxford

Theresa Mullane, Senior Primary Inspector, Richmond-upon-Thames

Dee Reid, Senior Lecturer, Oxford Brookes University

Contents

Acknowledgements

I am very grateful to all contributors for the generous sharing of ideas that made it possible to compile this book. My thanks, too, to Carolyn Beale for designing the photocopiable materials, and to David Leithead for the final illustrations. Photographs on page 54 are courtesy of Rowan White Photographic and Bournemouth Tourism.

A volume of this sort also requires substantial secretarial support. I am also very grateful to Sandy Williams and Jackie Hill, who typed the text, and Mary Hargreaves, who arranged the layout, with great patience and skill.

Samples of work from St Philip's Church and Community School, Warrington, and other individuals, are greatly appreciated.

INTRODUCTION
Extending the Range of Writing

The key stage 2 programme of study in *English in the National Curriculum* (GB. DFE 1995) focuses on the need to extend children's knowledge of the different kinds of writing, and to provide varied purposes and a range of readers so that children can learn about the choices open to them when they write. The section on writing begins as follows:

1. Range

a) Pupils should be given opportunities to write for varied purposes, understanding that writing is essential to thinking and learning and enjoyable in itself. They should be taught to use writing as a means of developing, organising and communicating ideas.

b) Pupils should be given opportunities to write for an extended range of readers, *eg the teacher, the class, other children, adults in school or community, imagined audiences*. They should write in response to a wide range of stimuli, including stories, plays and poems, their interests and experiences, and the activities of the classroom.

c) They should be taught to use the characteristics of different kinds of writing, *eg argument, commentary, narrative, dialogue*. The forms in which they write should include imaginative writing, *eg stories, poems, dialogues, drama scripts, diaries*; and non-fiction, *eg reports, instructions, explanations, notes, letters*. They should be taught to use features of layout and presentation.

GB.DFE, 1995

While few may disagree with these aims, many will wonder where to begin. This book aims to help put the key stage 2 Orders into practice by providing a framework for writing and by suggesting activities to help you develop your classroom work. It will help you as you plan:

 ◆ language activities that can help you develop schemes of work;

 ◆ a whole-school writing policy;

 ◆ in-service activities for school and year group meetings;

 ◆ meetings with parents about their child's writing development.

There are certain things that this book does not aim to do. It does not look in detail at spelling, punctuation or handwriting. It also does not deal directly with children who have special educational needs or with children learning English as an additional language. However, much that is said will help the teaching of all of these.

PRINCIPLES
Developing Effective Writing

Writing choices

Writing is about making choices. Each time we write we have to choose the most appropriate words and the best way to organise those words. As experienced adult writers, we make these *what* and *how* choices according to what we are writing about, who we are writing for and why we are writing.

From an early age, children begin to learn the different ways in which people around them use writing. By watching, listening and, later, by reading, they can learn how writing gets things done; how it informs, amuses or angers people; how it helps organise people's lives and how it brings people together. They see relationships between reading, writing and speech. Notes, for example, are written while people talk on the telephone; letters between family and friends may be read aloud and talked about while they are being written; stories are heard on tape, watched on video and played with on screen as well as being read silently or aloud. Writing is much more than the act of putting pen to paper. It is much more than knowing how to spell and use capital letters (though these are important). In the world outside school, writing is part of complex language and social events, and each community has rules about how writing is used to achieve its various purposes.

This book aims to help teachers provide children with experiences of writing events – like writing letters and instructions; or composing stories and reports – so that they can understand the choices that a writer faces and gain competence as effective writers.

What is an effective writer?

Children who are learning to write effectively are working out – through experience of talking, reading, and writing – the kinds of language required by different writing tasks. When we write, we use language to get things done: to convey feelings and attitudes; to sort out what we know; to pass on information; to change people's opinions; to exchange ideas and so on. For every writing **purpose** (to argue, persuade, inform, explain, amuse, report, etc.) and for every writing **audience** (friends, parents, consumers, etc.) there are choices about the best and most appropriate language structures and vocabulary to use. The structures and vocabulary choices combine to make up specific **forms** of writing – recipes, lists, advertisements, lectures, reports and so on.

Sometimes the links between purpose, audience and language form are obvious: a recipe format is generally appropriate to inform someone how to cook a dish; a list is best for the class register. However, there is flexibility in choice, especially once you move away from specific tasks like cooking towards less easily defined activities like expressing your feelings. By exploring and experimenting with these choices through language tasks that achieve a range of purposes, children will develop competence and confidence in writing.

In order to make judgements about a child's development as a writer, we need to ask, for each piece of writing, how they have tried to use language to meet the purpose in hand and how they have adapted their writing for their audience. It can be difficult to recognise the achievements – especially if a child's spelling and punctuation are not conventional. But when teachers focus on 'what is going right' and children themselves start talking about the language choices that work, then they can aim for new levels of writing competence.

This brings us to the important question *How do you extend a child's writing*? Stories, for instance, are often adequately written but they stop short of hoped-for levels. Recognising what is working in a story, and taking it further, require a more focused approach to the way language works. The Practical Activities in this book aim to provide some of that focus, and recommend ways of taking children's writing further forward.

Purpose and audience: who reads what is written?

Purpose and audience are two sides of the same coin. As well as providing children with a range of different purposes for writing, teachers need to provide them with a range of readers. Unless you know who you are writing for (at least in general terms) it is hard to decide how best to achieve a particular writing purpose. Very often in schools the reader needs to be the teacher or a classmate, but not exclusively. Parents, children in other schools, younger children, and adults in the community can become readily accessible audiences. Information technology can play an increasingly important role here in reaching new audiences.

There are also many possibilities for audiences in imagined worlds, and the Classroom Activities include a number of examples of these. In the *Letters* activity, for example, one idea is to take the familiar tale of *The Pied Piper of Hamelin* and ask children to explore the different types of letters that would be sent to or from diffferent characters: the mayor, the Pied Piper, local millers and so on. Comparable examples could be devised for many other areas of the curriculum.

When new audiences are found, and especially when those audiences respond, children's writing will change as they begin to understand the effects of their language choices on others. It is particularly helpful if intended readers are able to respond to early drafts. (Examples of drafts and responses are given in the section on the Writing Process.) Some key stage 2 class teachers ask children to write stories for younger children who comment on initial story ideas and react to drafts, as well as enjoying the finished products. One such writer commented:

> '*I have learned this term that writing is hard work... you have a really good feeling when you get it right*' (National Writing Project, 1989).

Purpose and form: what different kinds of writing are there?

It sounds fine in theory to refer to a writer's choices and recommend teaching different varieties for different audiences, but the choices can seem overwhelming. Many have tried to simplify writing in binary terms, such as *fiction* and *non-fiction* or even *creative* and (presumably) *not creative*.

Over the years, a number of more useful classifications have been developed. Unfortunately, the wide range of terms used (narrative, chronological, description, report, etc.) has left many feeling confused and uncertain about the variety of writing choices available.

There may not be agreement about the best way to divide up writing, but there is consensus that there are broad categories of writing with associated language features. For each of these, there are a number of characteristic *forms*. For example, a written argument is most likely to come in the form of a letter, debate, protest banner, leaflet or newspaper article. Each of these forms could be associated with other kinds of writing. A letter, for instance, is very flexible in the purposes it can achieve. At the same time, one form (eg a newspaper) will contain many different kinds of writing.

The Practical Activities in this book are organised according to different forms of writing, and some bring out the multiple roles that particular forms can play. For example, the *Letters* activity begins with children collecting and sorting a mass of letters in order to find out how many functions letters can have and how particular characteristics (eg openings and endings) vary according to the purpose.

Classifications of writing tend to 'leak' -- ie there are areas of overlap. They can also result in certain types of text getting insufficient attention. Poetry, too, is a form with many different purposes and yet with unique structures. The *Poetry* activity is designed to show children what poetry is and where it can be used. The starting point of all the activities is to show children the possibilities of writing so that they can become effective communicators in a variety of situations.

What are the characteristics of different types of writing?

If we want children to gain control of the different types of writing, we need to know how texts are structured, at least in broad terms. Below are a few of the features identified with seven different types of writing, based largely on the *Writing Frames* developed by Lewis and Wray (1995). It is not an exhaustive list and many written texts contain more than one type.

Most importantly, it is not intended as a teaching model. Children should read, discuss and write different types of text because of the communicative purposes they want to achieve, not because they are working through a checklist of written varieties. Once they have a specific purpose for writing, though, a framework can help a teacher to guide children's attention to the structures of language that will make their writing most effective.

TYPES OF TEXT AND TYPICAL FEATURES

TEXT TYPE	EXAMPLES	TYPICAL TEXT STRUCTURE	TYPICAL LANGUAGE CHARACTERISTICS
Recount	account of visit or historical event	*chronological* scene-setting sequence of events closing statement	past tense time markers (*when, then, finally*) focus on individuals (*Queen Victoria, the Prime Minister*) use of action words (*ordered, discovered*)
Report	textbook descriptions in science and humanities	*non- chronological* opening general statement (*The solar system is made up of...*) technical elaboration of category description of category	present tense focus on groups of things illustrations and diagrams sections, headings and different print-sizes use of technical language use of 'be' and 'have' verbs
Explanation	how things work; life cycles	*chronological* introductory statement logically organised steps (*when, that, then, this*)	present tense markers of time or cause (*when, because*) use of action vocabulary diagrams and illustrations
Procedures	instructions to make something	*chronological* statement of goal materials/requirements sequence of steps	present tense or imperatives use of times markers (*then, after*) focus on non-specific person (*you*) mainly action words diagrams and illustrations
Persuasion	protest against school uniform	*non-chronological* opening position statement series of points summary and restatement	present tense, questions and imperatives modal verbs (*may, should, can*) causal connectives (*because, therefore*) generic subjects (*children, teachers*)
Argument	should marbles be banned in the playground ?	*non-chronological* opening statement of issue arguments for and against summary and conclusion	present tense causal and contrastive connectives (*because, on the other hand*) generic subjects (*children, parents*) 'mental process' verbs (*feel, think*)
Narrative	fairy tale	*chronological* opening setting the scene characters, actions, events complication resolution coda (*eg moral message*)	past tense dialogue developed scene and characters descriptive vocabulary

What are the children writing about?

Amid all the talk of processes, purposes, audiences and text forms, it's easy to forget about the **content** – what are children writing about and how much do they know about it?

A text, especially a non-fiction one, can often fail because the child does not know enough about a topic. Halliday (1978) talks about the *field* of writing – the what, who, when, how, why and where of the subject. Knowledge of the field involves access to a topic's vocabulary and how to use it. Take an argument in favour of a zebra crossing, for example. Without an extensive vocabulary it may contain repetitions and deviations and appear poorly argued even though the structure of the text is well-organised. The writing of non-fiction texts in particular needs to begin with a lot of talk and brainstorming about the topic.

Choice of content is also very important. What do you do about stereotyped characters recurring in a child's writing or a well-written but excessively violent story from a ten-year-old? Such questions raise issues about the need for children to become critical readers of what they as well as others write. Writing is a *social* practice and children, like adults, have responsibilities as writers, and have to consider what, in a particular situation, it is appropriate and acceptable to write *about*. (Whether these issues should be pursued further with individuals is, of course, a pastoral question.)

What gets taught about writing in different subject areas?

Writing is a part of all curriculum areas both in its role as an aid to learning and in the various written forms expected in different subjects.

Writing *for* learning has perhaps been undervalued in the past, yet it plays a significant role in, for example:

- ◆ remembering ideas through note-taking and list-making;

- ◆ organising information using strategies such as story-boards, planning webs, labelling diagrams or sorting arguments into 'for' and 'against';

- ◆ reflecting on learning itself, for example through learning journals or writing logs.

Writing in different subject areas involves children understanding the range of written forms available and selecting the most appropriate one. Debates can become heated over whether certain types of writing are better suited to different subject areas – Is a poem appropriate in maths? Should narrative be used in science?

For some, failure to use a report form for a science experiment is thought to encourage lack of precision in observation (eg *'the liquid bubbled away happily for ages'*), and loss of objectivity (eg *'I loved the way it smelled'*). But others argue that children who are allowed to use a familiar text structure, like narrative, can display their understanding of an experiment which they would be unable to do if using less familiar text structures. The response to these arguments usually lies somewhere in the middle. Scientific understanding should not become slave to one written format but subject-specific genres need to be introduced *showing what they can do for organising ideas*.

Some kinds of writing used in different subject areas are unlikely to be read often by children and even more rarely read aloud and talked about. In the Practical Activities looking at Report Writing, there are suggestions for ways of 'scaffolding' reports through asking questions about the organisation of a text. Scaffolds like these can help children with all kinds of writing tasks.

How do writers write?

Writing is a complex process, and most adults have difficulties writing at least some of the time (ask any teacher!). Since the focus is often on *'what'* to write, the *'how'* to write sometimes gets forgotten.

All texts go through a process of creation but the details of that process vary. A note passed in class might be quickly written with almost no development; a script for a class assembly might, on the other hand, be planned for some weeks, drafted and redrafted even up to the last minute. Roald Dahl wrote about story writing like this: *'I write all my stories with pencils that have a rubber on the end, ...I rewrite each page several times. I go on doing this until I can't do any better.'*

Various points in the development of a piece of writing can be identified and developed with children. The programmes of study for writing (GB.DFE, 1995) describe the writing process under key skills as consisting of: planning, drafting, revising, proof-reading and presenting. This is not a fixed series of stages, and different texts will take more or less time at each point in the process, but it provides a useful overview of a writer's behaviour. For each stage, we can identify different strategies that we use, eg generating ideas, trying out different openings, rewriting the conclusion, and tidying up the spelling and punctuation. There is a more detailed description of the Writing Process on pages 16 to 25.

Research and experience have shown that children have little awareness of the processes involved in the creation of texts, and need to be *shown explicitly* what writers do. Children's attention to the different stages in the production of a text can be developed by, for example:

- ♦ discussing what authors do when they write;

- ♦ showing examples of drafts from published authors;

- ♦ recording the 'history' of one piece of writing in folders or on wall displays;

- ♦ writing with the children yourself and talking about what you do.

Different stages in the development of a piece of writing imply different criteria for success and consequently different responses from the teacher. In judging an early planning draft for, say, a *Guide to Local Playgrounds* you might focus on the use of maps; what constitutes appropriate play equipment; accuracy of information, appropriate terminology and so on. At a later stage, headings and layout might be discussed, and at an even later draft, spelling and handwriting/typing might be focused on. Once children know how their work will be judged at each stage they should find it easier to focus on the different demands of the writing activity and on the skills required. More is said about assessing effective writing in the final section of this booklet – assessment is both the place to begin and the place to end.

If the various drafts are put together at the end, a child has a history of her/his own development as a writer for one task and it is this explicit experience of writing behaviour that helps develop effective writers. One Year 5 child commented on the rewards of learning about the craft of writing:

'I like doing drafts about stories because when you are doing your second draft you can get different ideas and ... you usually find your story gets better and better every time. Editing also gets your story better because people find mistakes and if you miss a fault they might see it. (National Writing Project, 1989)

One effect of this approach to writing is that there will be more work done in preparing each writing task and, consequently, fewer different tasks overall. Curriculum planning for writing involves finding a balance between exploring different forms and functions of writing and exploring how any one text can be fully developed.

How are writing and speaking linked?

The three main strands of the English curriculum – writing, reading and speech – although separated in the DFE Orders for English (1995) are closely intertwined and often inseparable. In addition, new technology continually blurs the distinctions between speaking and writing. Television, tape recordings, e-mail, fax, and no doubt more to be invented, introduce new language variants which are often more familiar to children than to adults!

Writing is often described in terms of its differences from speech, and children's writing errors are often seen as resulting from a lack of awareness of such differences. In many of the comparisons of speaking and writing, there is a tendency to compare planned, fully revised, formal writing with spontaneous face-to-face conversation where there are significant differences between the two modes. Written and spoken language do have certain specialised functions and both speech and writing have developed their own characteristic language features. So, for example, legal documents sound strange spoken aloud and, comparably, face-to-face conversations are hard to write. However, it is more helpful to focus on the language choices appropriate to particular communications rather than argue about differences. For example, a school textbook (written) and a prepared talk in assembly (spoken) need to be well organised and integrated, of a certain length and using Standard English. By comparison, a shopping list (written) and informal chat (spoken) need less organisation and less regard for formal conventions or Standard English.

To give an example of another set of choices, a recipe (written) and football commentary (spoken) need to be very accurate and detailed about the information. In contrast, a limerick (written) and TV commercial (spoken) might focus more on rhyme and word play than on factual content. If children learn about the choices involved in both speech and writing they will find out what language can do and when particular kinds language are most appropriate.

As well as opportunities for discussing what will be written, many classroom activities for developing writing also offer opportunities for looking at spoken variations. One advantage of this is that children's experiences of spoken variants will be far more extensive than their experience of written forms and their understanding of variety in speech can help them to understand variety in writing. For example, written instructions for making something have parallels in television demonstrations of how to make or do something. Both have very similar language characteristics – eg chronological sequence of steps and use of present tense or imperatives. But they may differ in specific ways too, such as the need for labelled diagrams or illustrations to accompany writing when the materials cannot actually be seen by the viewer.

How are reading and writing linked?

Writing and reading also tend to get separated in the school curriculum and yet they, too, are inextricably linked. Letters are usually written in response to ones that have been received; professional writers usually begin by reading in order to get the feel for the structure of a planned text, and so on. The links seem obvious between what is read and what is written and yet it is not clear how children's reading of different texts affects their ability to develop different types of writing, nor how their writing affects their subsequent reading. Some children may be able to pick up the language structures specific to text types without explicit teaching (like 'catching' spelling, some can 'catch' language structures). But probably, for most, explicit attention to what is read or written is necessary. Children need to read as writers, and to write as readers.

Some examples of what this might mean in practice include:

- ♦ reading activities that encourage children to look closely at writing and writers – eg book-reviewing (non-fiction and fiction) or interviews with others about reading preferences;

- ♦ collaborative writing activities in which writers have immediate feedback from a writing partner;

- ♦ reading aloud a range of text-types;

- ♦ activities which encourage children to focus on text structure – eg rewriting an information booklet for younger children.

In the Practical Activities, many examples are given of books relevant to developing different varieties of writing. Newspapers, television, video, radio and the Internet are also sources of forms of literacy in its widest sense. The 'writing lessons' described here try to help children explore the many and varied opportunities that writing and reading can provide.

What role does technology play?

One of the roles of IT is to enhance learning in all areas of the curriculum alongside the development of specific IT capability skills. Although there are few references to the use of IT in *English in the National Curriculum* (GB. DFE, 1995), there are significant opportunities for its use in enabling children to develop as effective writers. It is a powerful tool that can be used to support and illuminate the writing process. Much of the good practice acquired through the use of IT also carries over into the use of the more traditional tool, the pencil.

Each invention, from papyrus to word processors, has affected the what and how of writing. Photocopying allows drafts to be discussed and worked on without damage to the original. Information technology has helped to develop a range of writing activities and has widened the choices available to writers. For example:

♦ desktop publishing enables children to explore more easily a whole range of formats, such as posters and newspapers, and to integrate words and images;

♦ word processing influences the way writers draft and redraft and allows finished pieces of writing to be attractively presented and circulated in multiple copies;

♦ different fonts, layouts and settings can be experimented with and their effects on the reader evaluated;

♦ concept keyboards open doors for children, especially those with learning difficulties;

♦ spell-check programmes can be used to help proof-reading;

♦ specific programmes can be used to help introduce children to writing formats, such as tabulating information, or labelling diagrams;

♦ word processors can facilitate collaborative writing;

♦ CD-ROMs provide new ways of finding, manipulating and presenting information;

♦ children can reach new audiences and explore a whole new form of written communication through e-mail, where the conventions are still in the making.

Above all, the use of IT establishes a different relationship between the writer and the text, taking away the direct physical link and giving the text the professional appearance of print media. Particularly for those who have difficulty with the physical process of writing, it can take some of the struggle out of learning to write.

There are numerous programmes that offer relevant opportunities to aid the writing process.

Examples:	Word processing	*Word, Writeon, Flexiwrite*
	Desktop publishing	*Publisher*
	Simulations	*Rescue/Hazard, Newsroom*
	Information handling	*Clipboard, Flexidata, Clarisworks,* CD-ROMs

What messages are we giving children about writing?

In the Practical Activities section that follows there is an underlying picture of a classroom which supports the development of effective writing. It includes at least some of these features:

- ♦ a range of materials – pens, pencils, rubbers, different sized paper, book-binding equipment, word processor, desktop publishing and other programmes and many materials to suit different tasks;

- ♦ reading areas including a wide range of text forms;

- ♦ teachers and pupils talking and writing *about* writing and writers;

- ♦ children exercising choice over what happens before, during and after writing;

- ♦ children experimenting with different forms and functions of writing;

- ♦ children working together on texts;

- ♦ teachers writing alongside children;

- ♦ writing leaving the classroom – eg letters being sent; story books being given to key stage 1 classes; information going to its intended audience;

- ♦ examples on display showing a range of different forms of writing;

- ♦ displays showing the processes of writing (eg drafts);

- ♦ a bin for abandoned drafts!

Finally, it is always helpful to remember that a teacher or parent's view of the writing lesson may not be the same as that of the child. Children very quickly pick up the real agenda – the 'ground rules' for writing in class. You may have designed a stimulating activity writing recipes for Tudor feasts, but if the only comments on their finished work are about handwriting and spelling, children will draw their own conclusion about the important aspects to focus on when writing. Before developing activities for writing, try asking children *their* views.

What makes a piece of writing effective?

Who writes?

Why do you write?

Who do you write for?

What kinds of writing do you not enjoy?

What helps you while you are writing?

What kind of comments do you find helpful?

(There is a photocopiable master based around these ideas on pages 12-13.)

The answers will be revealing. Often children focus on neatness and spelling as the main criteria for effective writing; many find it hard to talk about the different types of writing they do and the most common answer for 'Who do you write for?' is 'the teacher'. When the focus is on extending the *range* of writing, answers like these underline the need for new purposes, audiences and forms of writing and, perhaps most importantly, point out the need to introduce and explain to children the writing choices available. It is by gaining control over such choices that they will become increasingly effective writers.

The Writing Process

- How do you plan your writing?
- Do you write drafts so that you can get your ideas onto paper quickly?
- What helps you while you are writing?
- How do you like to be helped with your writing?
- What sort of comments do you find helpful?
- Do you share your writing with anyone?
- Do you read other children's writing? How do you help them to improve?
- Does the speed and look of your writing vary?
- Do you like to illustrate your writing or present it in different ways?

My feelings about writing

There are lots of different kinds of writing eg stories, letters, poems, diairies, lists, reports, invitations, recipes, advertisments, and many more.

Who do you see writing? What and why are they writing? Who are they writing for?

List all the different kinds of writing you do.

Shade in or underline your favourite kinds of writing.

If there is any kind of writing you don't enjoy, put a circle round it.

Why do you write? Who do you write for? Who reads your writing?

Where do you like to do your writing?
What do you like to write with?
What do you like to write on?

What do you use to check or correct your spelling? Do you like to write on your own or with others?

What do you like about writing?
What do you not like about writing?
What makes a piece of writing good?
What makes a piece of writing poor?

Rate yourself as a writer

How I see myself

poor   average   good   excellent

How my teacher sees me

poor   average   good   excellent

TEACHING WRITING
The Role of the Teacher

Before children embark on any form of writing, teachers and children need to consider

- the purpose and audience

- the intended outcomes

- the learning objectives

When teachers are aware of the steps involved in the writing process, they can provide support at relevant points and enable children to learn from the process itself.

The section on the Writing Process looks at planning, drafting and revision, and the Practical Activities section presents a range of forms of writing – letters, diaries, dialogues, stories, etc. – using approaches devised by teachers for use in key stage 2 classrooms. While the precise approaches vary, there is an implicit assumption that the teacher takes an active part in supporting children's writing, as exemplified in the chart overleaf. The following chart uses instructions as a focus, but can be applied to other types of writing.

Obviously, teaching any type of writing does not have to follow this model rigidly. The children's prior knowledge and experience will influence which particular aspects of writing are explained and modelled. For instance, one might focus on descriptions in stories, leaving other aspects of story writing to be explored with the children on other occasions. The degree of guidance to support children's choices will also vary. Schools and teachers will need to make their own decisions about the breadth and depth of coverage they give to a particular area, and decide an appropriate timescale.

A MODEL FOR TEACHING WRITING

Stage 1 PREPARATION	Stage 2 FOCUS AND DISCUSSION	Stage 3 DEMONSTRATION AND PRACTICE	Stage 4 KNOWLEDGE IN CONTEXT	Stage 5 GROUP, PAIR OR INDIVIDUAL WRITING

Teacher
 	
• selects type of writing in relation to curriculum planning, *eg procedures in relation to maths or DT*
 	
• gathers representative collection of published examples
 	
• familiarises self with particular features of the type of writing
 	
• considers implications for planning and teaching
	Teacher
	
	• selects models from collection, *eg receipts, instruction manuals*
	
	• introduces them to children and draws attention to ;
	  – format
	  – layout
	  – organisation
	  – features of language
	
	Children find out other examples *eg rules of a game, instructions for model making*
	
	Teacher and children compare examples, looking for similarities and differences and discuss the purpose and effect of illustrations and the use of diagrams, symbols, etc.
		Teacher raises awareness and develops knowledge of instructional language through the following :
		
		i) demonstration, using a simple text, highlighting :
		  – organisational features
		  – key word and phrases
		
		ii) repetition: children working in pairs, using a similar text, repeat the activity
		
		iii) discussion and evaluation: teacher and children discuss highlighted features, children explain reason for choices
		
		iv) practice: children working in pairs construct a series of guidelines for the writing of instructions or procedures to be displayed and referred to
			In the context of the curriculum focus, teacher constructs a text with a group or whole class, *eg rules for a maths game they have devised, instructions for a model made in DT*
			
			Teacher again models the process, discussing
			  – language features
			  – organisational devices
			  – the place of illustrations, and referring to the guidelines produced by the children.
			Teachers and children plan and draft a new text, children working in pairs
			
			On completion, children discuss, compare and evaluate texts
			
			Teacher and children discuss learning outcomes
				• Teacher acts as guide and consultant
				
				• Children as experts, plan and draft texts
				
				• Drafts trialled by other children, *eg instructions are followed*
				
				• Drafts evaluated in relation to purpose
				
				• Revisions made
				
				• Final texts presented

THE WRITING PROCESS
Planning, Drafting and Revising

Pupils should be given opportunities to plan, draft and improve their work on paper and on screen and to discuss and evaluate their own and other writing.

(GB.DFE, 1995)

This section considers steps in the writing process. It examines what is meant by the terms commonly in use, and suggests a way of modelling the writing process and developing pupils' opportunities to improve their own work.

Planning

The success of the writing will be significantly influenced by the initial stimulus and planning. At this stage the writer should be clear about:

- ◆ purpose of writing

- ◆ intended audience

- ◆ features of the form eg ingredients of a myth, structure of an argument, features of persuasive writing, conventions of playscripts, etc.

Drafting

The skills of drafting and revising need to be developed in the context of the range of writing, eg poems, stories, letters, instructions, etc. A 'draft' is a piece of (usually continuous) structured text written in response to thoughts and ideas outlined in the planning stage. A draft may have to stand as a final copy if no opportunity is available for review. In real life, most often, there is an opportunity to review a first draft and to make amendments. **Drafting is not rewriting to get a neater and neater copy.**

Revising

Initial thoughts developed and written in a continuous structured text may not communicate exactly the intended meaning for the reader. Conveying the appropriate tone and style for the intended audience may need adjustment. For these reasons, amendments, deletions and additions often need to be made.

It is not possible to carry a whole text in the head and to decide at the end what needs improving or changing. A text needs working through bit by bit for decisions to be made in relation to content, use of language and structure.

Teachers or other readers will always need to respond to content, use of language and structure in order to move the development of the writer forward in terms of communicating meaning. Whether this is done as a result of an individual conference with the writer, as written messages/queries to the writer or as a group response will be decisions for individual teachers to make. In order to develop awareness of the kind of questioning that would help a writer, the guide on page 20 may be of use.

Proof reading and editing

These skills need to be taught in the context of the process of writing. However, it is difficult to produce an initial draft, then immediately check for mistakes in punctuation and spelling and anticipate the interpretation of meaning for a reader. This 'reading for revisions' is more effectively approached if the writer has put the draft aside even for a short period of time.

Demonstrating the process

For children to be clear about the writing process and for them to be able to respond to each other's work, they need to see the process exemplified.

Planning

- There are many different approaches to planning, and there may be some that you are particularly comfortable with. Planning 'webs' are useful for brainstorming ideas; 'bags of words' help to focus on the language used. Where a number of issues are to be covered (in information writing, for example) it may be helpful to use headings, which themselves need to be thought out carefully.

- Demonstrate planning by using the children's ideas. Remember to establish purpose, audience and other important factors before taking plans further, *eg a letter inviting parents to a presentation or exhibition.*

Drafting

- Working collaboratively with the class or group, demonstrate how to compose a piece of writing, referring to the plans.

- Articulate your thoughts aloud eg 'I think I ought to let them know what this letter is about first.'

- Invite pupils to help eg Which idea comes next? How do you think we should say that? Do you think we should start a new paragraph for this? Do any of our other ideas go with this one?

- Talk to the group about the tone and style of the letter, and keep reminding everyone who the readers will be.

Revising

♦ Demonstrate the process by working on a first draft. After a break from the writing, ask the group if you should change anything before taking it to another group or person for review, eg Do you think they will understand what we meant here? Have we checked that we've said everything?

♦ Invite another group or person to read the draft text through a bit at a time and invite questions and comments (see guide on page 20).

♦ Show how amendments, additions, etc. are best written on a separate page with corresponding symbols or numbers to indicate their placement in the text. Agree conventions for this with the group.

♦ Finally, check for unnecessary repetitions, and for accuracy of spelling and punctuation.

♦ Show how to write the letter (or poem/report/instructions, etc.) incorporating revisions and showing the conventions of layout.

Issues for writing which cannot be reviewed

♦ Take as an example a piece of writing (your own or somebody else's) which had to be a good fair copy and which was not amended in any way, eg a message, a piece of private writing like a diary entry, a completed form.

♦ Talk about the considerations and thought processes relating to that example, eg by considering how accuracy of punctuation, spelling, content, use of language and presentation had to be monitored all at the same time.

Using the process

Children may work individually, in pairs, or in small groups to undertake some or all of these activities in relation to a piece of work.

In the context of a real purpose and a defined audience (known or unknown), the children should now be ready to draft a piece of writing, referring to their initial plans. You may ask them to write an opening paragraph, a portion of an intended complete text or a complete text in itself.

Remind the children that they will

♦ be able to amend the writing and check accuracy of punctuation and spelling, so they can devote their undivided attention to communicating their thoughts and ideas well;

♦ need a double page spread so that the draft can be written on one side and amendments and additions on the opposite page;

♦ need to check their plans as they go along to guide them through the writing.

After a break from writing the initial draft, the children read through their own writing *as if they were another reader*. This will help them to perceive the writing from another reader's point of view and to make amendments.

- ◆ When they make amendments or additions, remind them to use the code of symbols or numbers to indicate placement in the text.

Children now invite another reader (teacher/peer) to go through their writing bit by bit according to the guide on page 20.

- ◆ If the reader reviews the piece of work in the absence of the writer, questions or comments or messages can be written on the page opposite the first draft.

Children write amendments, additions or deletions using the agreed symbols or numbers to indicate where they will be added in the original draft.

- ◆ Reassure everyone that deletions can be made on the first draft.

- ◆ If an individual is daunted by writing additions and amendments because of his/her developmental stage, a scribe can write these so that he/she is not disadvantaged.

When the children have finished reviewing and amending their work, proof reading for punctuation and spelling and editing unnecessary repetitions, decide whether the writing is to be passed on to another person or published or displayed. If not, **there is no need to rewrite**.

Draw attention to any conventions of layout or presentation associated with a particular from of writing, eg instructions, explanation, letters etc.

If the writing is to be shared with a wider audience, ask the children to write out the draft incorporating amendments, additions, etc. in their appropriate places as the text is being written.

In supporting children to improve the quality of their writing, identify particular needs with individuals or groups, eg variety of sentence beginnings, sentence lengths, reported speech. Directing children to literature to see how authors tackle these aspects of language is a very useful strategy within the process of drafting and revising.

Extension

- ◆ Re-present a draft of narrative as dialogue or playscript.

- ◆ Investigate appropriate ways of presenting a final copy by looking at books, brochures, etc.

- ◆ Following a teaching point or discussion, ask pupils to make their own checklists/prompts to aid revisions.

GUIDE TO RESPONDING TO WRITING

♦　　　Read through the whole piece, whether it is a paragraph or a completed piece of work. This will give you an idea of what it is about.

♦　　　Go through it then sentence by sentence or a bit at a time. Talk about anything that seems important. Make appreciative remarks.

MAKE COMMENTS OR ASK QUESTIONS ABOUT THE IDEAS AND WHAT THE WRITER IS TELLING YOU

♦　　　This is interesting, can you tell me a bit more about this bit?

♦　　　I'm wondering about this.

♦　　　I don't quite understand this. Is this what you mean?

♦　　　Can you explain a bit more about it?

♦　　　Is this what you're saying?

♦　　　I'm not sure I agree with what you're saying here because...

♦　　　Do you think you should have mentioned ...?

♦　　　Do certain ideas or points go together?

MAKE COMMENTS OR ASK QUESTIONS ABOUT THE WAY THE WRITER HAS USED WORDS AND SENTENCES

♦　　　I like this word/these words/this image ...

♦　　　Are there other words you could use to make this clearer/livelier..?

♦　　　Are some words repeated? Do you need to find alternatives for, eg 'said', 'got'?

♦　　　Do any sentences need changing or linking together?

♦　　　Do all your sentences start in the same way?

♦　　　Does this sound right?

♦　　　Are you writing in the past or present tense all the way through?

PROOF READING

♦　　　Do you think there are any mistakes in spelling? Do you need to check with a dictionary or spell checker?

♦　　　Do you need to check punctuation? Read it through again.

CHILD'S WORK – Purpose

Purpose.

What am I writing?

A factual piece of information ~ a description

of the American garden at Biddulf Grange.

Who is my reader?

A visitor to the classroom because it will go on

display or in my portfolio.

Why am I writing?

To record what we learnt at Biddulf Grange

and to inform other people.

CHILD'S WORK – Notes

Next to a large ,ornamental pond with 20 15lb Mirror Carp. ✓
10 ft deep, ✓
Lily pads,
Weeping holly planted on 10ft rock, block and tackle
needed to lift rock.1860. ✓
Rock is Chatsworth gritstonefrom quarry at nearby
Troughstone Hill. ✓
Rhododendron bushes, James Bateman loved these and
azaleas. Both types of plant came first from North America. ✓
Two, Victorian cast iron benches (Coalbrook) 1846 with ✓
Lily of the Valley design, birds for the legs, price today ✓
£4000, ✓
Curved path around the lake, ✓
Most plants built on mounds, ✓
Pond has island in middle with weeping willow trees, ✓
 Bought expensive plants but also planted heather gathered
from nearby moor. ✓

There are male and female hollies, females
have berries and males don't. The female
was called Golden King and the male
was called Silver Queen. ✓

Planning

We collected together all the notes that the
class made during or after the visit.

CHILD'S WORK – Draft and Teacher's Comments

Biddulph Grange

As we left the Italian garden we entered the American garden. At the side of the garden there was a 10ft deep ornamental pond with 20,151lb Mirror carp and some lily pads. In the middle of the pond there was an island with weeping willow trees on. At the other side of the curved path there were two Victorian iron cast benches from Coalbrook Dale in (Coalbrook) 1846. They had a lily of the Valley design, birds for the legs and the price of them today would be £4,000 pounds each. Most of the plants were built on mounds, they were expensive plants but there was some Heathers gathered from a nearby moor. There is a (big) Weeping Holly on 10ft rock. They needed block and tackle to lift the rock in 1860. The rock is Chatsworth gritstone from a quarry at nearby Troughstone Hill. *James Bateman loved Rhododendron bushes and Azaleas both types of plants came from North America, which is where this garden got its name.

*1 There is a male holly called silver Queen and a female called Golden King. Male hollys don't have berries and females do.

for the book,

Can we think about changing some of the sentences around?

eg begun with Weeping willow trees....

big?

CHECKLIST FOR DRAFTING

Now that you have finished the first draft you need to check these things:

If you want to discuss your work with a reading partner at any stage, do so.

CONTENT

1. Read through your notes again and tick off all the information you have included in your text.

2. Look at the information you have not ticked off. Do you need to include that somewhere in your text?

3. Have you included enough description so that your reader knows what was in the garden and what it looked like? You could look at the pictures in our book or the postcards to help you remember.

LANGUAGE

1. Do all your sentences begin the same way?
(There is a....   I saw a....)
Beginning your sentences in a different way will change their structure and make them more interesting for your reader.
(Along the curved path grew....)
(Overhanging bushes lined the....)

2. Have you used some words many times?
(Garden ... pond ... saw ...)

SPELLING AND PUNCTUATION

1. Read your text carefully and pretend this is the first time you have seen it. Is there enough punctuation for your reader to understand the meaning and read it easily?

2. Read your text carefully just thinking about the look of the words. Underline any which you think may not be spelt correctly. Look them up in a dictionary.

FINALLY

If you think your work is finished and you feel happy with it, take it to a reading partner for a final proof reading before you publish it.

WELL DONE!

CHILD'S WORK – Final Version

Biddulph Grange.

As we left the Italian garden we entered the American garden. At the side of the garden there was a 10ft deep ornamental pond with 20, 15 lb Mirror Carp and some lily pads. In the centre of the pond you could see an island clustered with Weeping Willow trees. At the other side of the curved path were two, Victorian iron cast benches made in Coalbrook Dale in 1846. They had lily of the Valley design for the backs, birds for the legs. The price of them today would be £4,000 each. Most of the plants were expensive, and built on mounds, but there were some Heathers gathered from a nearby moor. There is a huge Weeping Holly on 10ft rock. They needed block and tackle to lift the rock in 1860. The rock is Chatsworth gritstone from a quarry at nearby Troughstone Hill. There is a male holly called Silver Queen and a female holly called Golden king. Male hollys don't have berries and females do. James Bateman loved Rhododendron bushes and Azaleas, both types of plant come from North America, which is where the garden got its name.

PRACTICAL ACTIVITIES

Letters

Letters can be written for a variety of audiences, for a variety of purposes. Work on writing letters is a particularly direct way of coming to grips with the importance of both these considerations and children often enjoy modifying their way of writing for specific readers in this context. The form of the letter can be studied along the way, and the scope for formal and informal letters allows consideration of issues of tone. If letters can be sent for a real purpose, children will have the reward of receiving a response and perhaps achieving other results through their writing.

Purpose

◆ to know that there are a variety of letter forms and that letters can vary in content, style and presentation

◆ to recognise that letters are written for a variety of purposes

◆ to study good models of letter writing, identifying, analysing and using conventions found in formal and informal letters, eg ways of setting them out and standard phrases used

◆ to write and respond to formal and informal letters with understanding of the relationship between the writer and the intended audience.

Preparation and organisation

◆ Class discussion and sorting activities leading to individual work or collaborative work in pairs or small groups. (There is a photocopiable master available to support this work on page 31.)

◆ Make a display of letters and envelopes which you and the children have collected and written to reinforce teaching points.

Timescale

◆ This unit of work may span one term.

Suggested sequence of activities

◆ Discuss letters which the children have sent or received. Why did they send letters and to whom? Do they think that the type of letter sent and received will change once they are adults?

◆ Collect and discuss as many different kinds of letters as possible. The children can investigate post coming into school or their homes and letters sent from school or their homes. Talk about why each letter has been sent (to thank, complain, provide information, request etc), the type of letter and its tone (business, personal, etc.), presentation (handwritten in pencil, biro or ink, typewritten, word-processed, faxed, etc.) and layout.

◆ Sort the letters into categories which the children agree upon. Ensure that the chosen categories allow for the study of, for example, different openings and endings, words and expressions which are particularly appropriate within a particular kind of letter, layout and organisation of content. The children can underline parts of photocopied letters and make notes if appropriate.

◆ Write individually, or in pairs or small groups, letters based on a well-known myth, tale or legend, eg *The Pied Piper of Hamelin*. Include tasks which allow the children to use the information in the story and extend it, and to explore different kinds of letters. Possibilities include letters of complaint from the shopkeepers to the Mayor and councillors about the rats, anxious letters from mothers or cooks, letters of blame from the citizens to the millers storing grain which attracts the rats, letters from the Pied Piper – first explaining his 'gift', then demanding money and then explaining why it was necessary to take the action he did. The task of writing letters from the Mayor or the Town Clerk to the Pied Piper will provide opportunities for the children to write very formal letters. The photocopiable master on page 31 gives children possible styles of arrangement, openings and endings. The children can take on the roles of different characters within the story and reply to letters sent to them.

◆ Make a display of letters and replies to them. Include plans, drafts and final copies.

Extension

◆ Write letters which are exchanged between fairy tale characters who share a predicament, eg the Beast and the Frog Prince.

◆ Write letters based around wordless texts, eg *Window* by Jeannie Baker.

◆ Write letters to the class teacher or parents about the term's work.

♦ Write letters seeking information about subjects, eg endangered species.

♦ Write letters responding to information, eg letters of protest about tree-felling.

♦ Maximise the opportunities provided by letters to write for a real audience, eg friends, teachers, people in the local or wider community, people in the world of work, clubs and organisations.

♦ Examine how letters move fiction along, eg *Cliffhanger* by J. Wilson.

♦ Look at samples of historical letters. Collect words or phrases that are not in common use today.

Text models

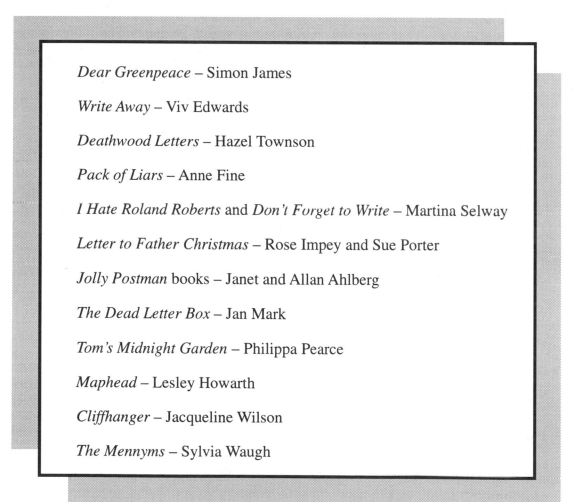

Dear Greenpeace – Simon James

Write Away – Viv Edwards

Deathwood Letters – Hazel Townson

Pack of Liars – Anne Fine

I Hate Roland Roberts and *Don't Forget to Write* – Martina Selway

Letter to Father Christmas – Rose Impey and Sue Porter

Jolly Postman books – Janet and Allan Ahlberg

The Dead Letter Box – Jan Mark

Tom's Midnight Garden – Philippa Pearce

Maphead – Lesley Howarth

Cliffhanger – Jacqueline Wilson

The Mennyms – Sylvia Waugh

Letters

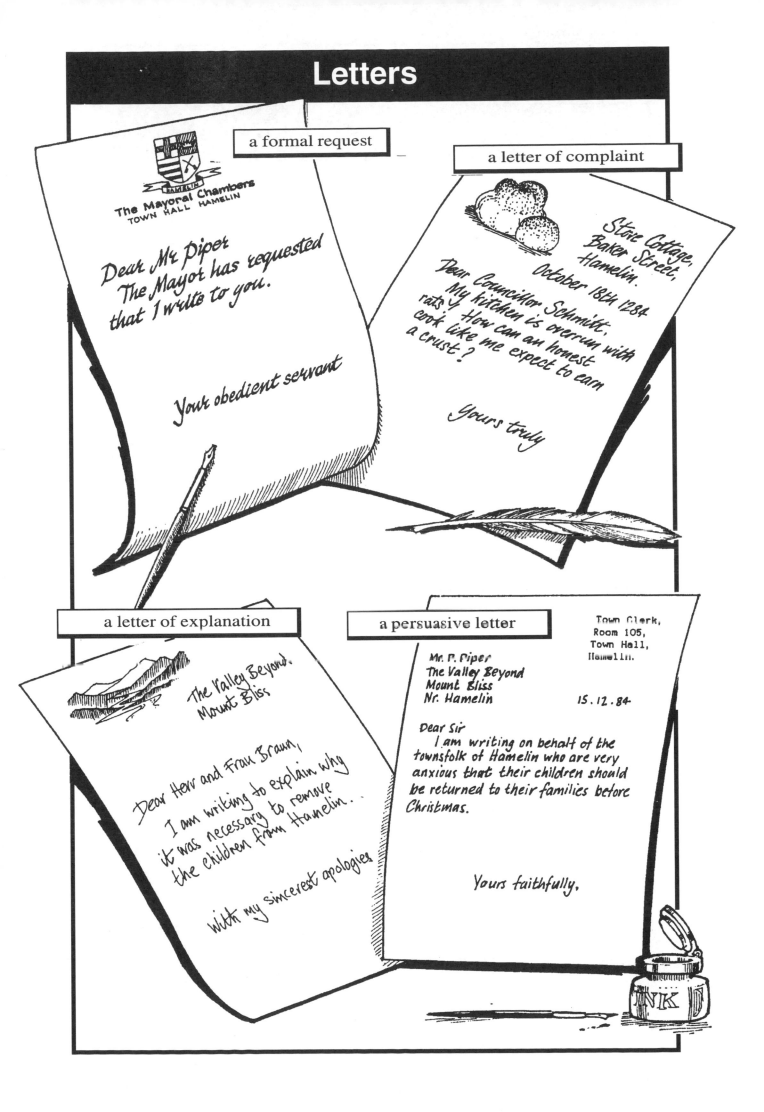

a formal request

The Mayoral Chambers
TOWN HALL HAMELIN

Dear Mr Piper
   The Mayor has requested
that I write to you.

          Your obedient servant

a letter of complaint

Stone Cottage,
Baker Street,
Hamelin.

October 18th 1284

Dear Councillor Schmitt,
   My kitchen is overrun with
rats! How can an honest
cook like me expect to earn
a crust?

          Yours truly

a letter of explanation

The Valley Beyond.
Mount Bliss

Dear Herr and Frau Braun,
   I am writing to explain why
it was necessary to remove
the children from Hamelin.

   With my sincerest apologies

a persuasive letter

Town Clerk,
Room 105,
Town Hall,
Hamelin.

Mr. P. Piper
The Valley Beyond
Mount Bliss
Nr. Hamelin   15.12.84

Dear Sir
   I am writing on behalf of the
townsfolk of Hamelin who are very
anxious that their children should
be returned to their families before
Christmas.

          Yours faithfully.

Dialogue and Playscripts

In a culture dominated by the moving image, many children visualise their stories as being dramatised, and need to learn the difference between this and presenting dialogue in narrative. Children will find the strengths of dialogue – its immediacy and liveliness – will improve their stories, and working on playscripts and dialogues together will help them to recognise the different conventions of drama and narrative, so that they can use dialogue to advantage in their stories.

Purpose

♦   to write and present dialogue in a variety of ways

♦   to re-present dialogue in other forms – comic strip, play, story, newspaper article

♦   to know that dialogue can convey information about character, story setting or action.

Preparation and organisation

♦   Whole class discussion moving to group, pair or individual writing tasks. (There is a photocopiable master to use with this unit of work on page 35.)

Timescale

♦   This unit on dialogue may span one term.

Suggested sequence of activities

♦   Discuss with the children ways in which speech can be written down . How can a joke, told orally, be re-presented on paper in different ways? For example, using speech bubbles, in comic strip form, as a play.

♦   Look at playscripts. Discuss elements of action that can be conveyed by dialogue *alone*, and consider the role of character lists, descriptions of set, stage directions (short descriptions in italics). Look at layout of dialogue. Group-read a selection of plays.

- Make a group/class guide on writing a good playscript – *A User's Guide to Play Writing*. This will ensure that the children discuss what makes a good play and can justify their choice of favourite plays, as well as helping them to focus on ways of using the conventions.

- Compare the layout of a playscript with a narrative poem containing dialogue, eg *Mummy, Oh Mummy* (anon) found in *Earthways Earthwise* – poems on conservation selected by Judith Nicholls. Discuss the dialogue – spoken words in written form. What does the dialogue reveal about the characters?

- Rewrite the poem so that it can be performed as a play. Discuss the differences between these ways of presenting the ideas, and how the dialogue provided clues for the stage directions, etc.

- Present part or all of the poem as a comic strip. Use speech bubbles for the dialogue, and pictures to tell the story. Is this an effective way of presenting the ideas?

- Redraft the poem as a story. Make sure that it is a mixture of dialogue and narrative. Look through books in the classroom or library to find words which can be used instead of *said*. This will avoid over-use of the word *said*. Is it possible to write a section of dialogue without using *said* or alternative phrases?

- Discuss the difference between direct and reported speech. The photocopiable master gives examples for you to draw upon. The children can then go on from this example to think of more claims which each season might make in support of his/her bid to remain firmly on the calendar. They can add more speech bubbles and complete the two columns containing direct and reported speech.

Extension

- Compare the story version of, eg, *James and the Giant Peach* by Roald Dahl with the play version by Roald Dahl/Richard George (Puffin).

- Read and discuss books which interweave narrative, dialogue in speech bubbles and pictures, eg *Jets*.

- Compare a story with a playscript, eg *The One That Got Away* by Jan Mark, and the playscript of the story in Ginn *New Reading 360 Plays*. Write a *Good Playscript Guide*.

- Select a passage from a book which contains dialogue. Rewrite it without using any dialogue. Maintain the storyline.

- Write down taped conversations.

♦ Write imagined conversations with book characters.

♦ Choose a moment in a story which the author does not describe but which must have happened. Ask the children to provide the missing text in play format.

♦ Find a story, written by a child, containing repetitive dialogue which fails to move the story along. With the child's permission, you and the class can work on photocopies of the story and improve it.

♦ Re-present on paper part of a debate which has taken place in the classroom, eg a debate on pollution. This activity may be a useful transition to some work on Reports (page 55).

Text models

Jets series A & C Black
    – narrative, dialogue in speech bubbles and pictures

Narrative poems with dialogue in:

   Conversation Piece in *Salford Road and Other Poems* – Gareth Owen

   The Walrus and the Carpenter – Lewis Carroll

   Dirty Beasts (a collection of poems) – Roald Dahl

   The Turbulent Term of Tyke Tyler – Gene Kemp
   (play version available)

Ginn *All Aboard* plays

Ginn *New Reading 360* plays

Oxford Primary English *Scripts and Poems for Reading Aloud*
                              – (series editor John Foster)

Dialogue

Direct Speech	Reported Speech
'People rely on me to save them money on their fuel bills!' exclaimed Summer. 'If I had to go, there would be no sliding, skating or sledging,' warned Winter.	Summer argued that people relied upon him to save them money on their fuel bills. Winter, on the other hand, made the point that he was needed for sliding, skating and sledging.

Diaries

As with letters, diaries may be written for a range of purposes and audiences. Work on diaries gives children the opportunity to consider chronological presentation of accounts, and to explore the combination of factual and personal information that is common to this type of writing.

Purpose

♦ to know there are a variety of diary forms and that these can vary in content, style and presentation

♦ to recognise that diaries are written for a variety of purposes

♦ to study good models of diary writing

♦ to write in diary form.

Preparation and organisation

♦ Collect as many examples as possible of different diary forms, eg your day-to-day diary, the school log, the diary of Anne Frank, the historical diaries of Captain Scott or Samuel Pepys. (There is a photocopiable master to use with this unit of work on page 39.)

Timescale

♦ This unit of work may span a term.

Suggested sequence of activities

♦ Show the children the range of diaries that you have, reading extracts as appropriate, and discuss with them the different purposes people have for keeping a diary.

♦ Look at the ways the diaries differ according to the purpose and audience. For example the day-to-day diary may have only a time and place entered, the reflective diary of Anne Frank is more concerned with how she feels, Scott's diary was written for the rescuers to find and he 'talks' to them through his entries. You could consider how they make different assumptions about what the reader already knows, and whether their tone is personal or impersonal.

♦ Look at the way the different diaries are written and guide the children to notice their characteristic features. You may wish to comment on such aspects as length of sentences, vocabulary, use of adjectives or adverbs.

♦ The children can now work with a partner to plan an entry for a day-to-day diary. They could do this for a well-known character from a traditional tale such as the giant in *Jack and the Beanstalk*. Alternatively, they could imagine the diary of an adult they know well.

♦ Read the story of *Super Dooper Jezebel* to the class. (If this is not available, you could base the work on the different diary entries that might have been written by Goldilocks, Father Bear and Baby Bear, or take three characters from a story you have read aloud to the class.)

♦ Give each child a copy of page 39 which shows entries from the diaries of the three main characters in the story. Use these to remind the children of the different characters and perceptions of the keeper, Jezebel and the teacher, and discuss the way these are reflected in their diaries. Discuss also the way the *purpose* of each diary affects the style in which it is written and think about further entries that each character would be likely to make. Working in pairs, the children can use the sheet to help them plan the continuation of the diary entries. They should then choose one of the characters and draft a diary entry, individually or with their partner.

♦ At this stage, children can share their drafts with a reader, responding to each other's work and making specific suggestions for revisions to content and/or language as appropriate. When the piece has been redrafted, it can be checked for presentational features such as spelling, punctuation and layout so that it can be put on display.

♦ The children could also read their entries to the class, adopting the tone of voice that they think appropriate to the character. Praise writers who have clearly identified with the character and point out how the *choice of language* as well as the way it is read out contribute to the success of their text.

♦ Make a display of the diary entries set around the book.

Extension

♦   Take a text of approximately 100 words from a published diary extract and one of 100 words from a descriptive passage in a work of fiction. Keep a tally of adjectives and adjectival phrases. What do you notice? What do you think is the reason for this?

♦   Make a similar comparison with a piece from an information reference book. What do you notice?

Text models

Diaries

Diary of Anne Frank

The Story of Tracy Beaker – Jacqueline Wilson

Mr Bean's Diary – Rowan Atkinson and Robin Driscoll

Diary of a Church Mouse – Graham Oakley

The Shorter Pepys
– edited by Robert Latham and William Matthews

Logs

Columbus

The Captain's Log in *Star Trek*

The Beagle's Log – (Darwin)

Diaries

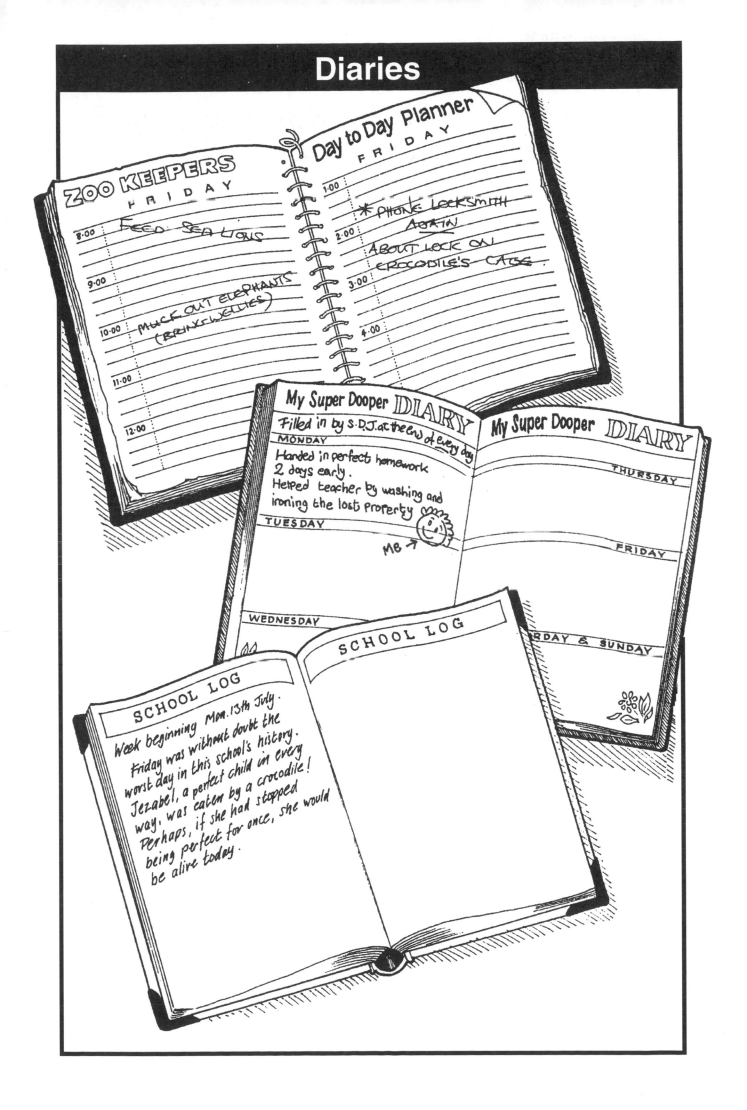

Making Notes

The ability to make good notes is one that will enhance children's learning right across the curriculum. It also has clear relevance to a variety of situations outside the classroom. Although note-taking is usually associated with factual text, children may enjoy learning to be methodical about notes in the context of fiction, too. The ability to write succinctly is a particular skill that will also be of value to children as they move on to key stage 3.

Purpose

♦ to develop note-making skills and the ability to write notes from text in an organised way

♦ to develop the skill of identifying key points by selecting relevant pieces of information and rejecting others

♦ to learn that notes can be written in a variety of ways

♦ to learn how notes facilitate the composition of text. (There is a possible link here with work in the *Reports* section, page 55.)

Preparation and organisation

♦ Whole-class discussion leading to teacher modelling of note-making task. Individual, pair or group note-making task – children work from photocopies of selected text. Children check the effectiveness of their notes through partner response activities.

♦ There is a photocopiable master available (see page 43).

Timescale

♦ This unit of work may span one term.

Suggested structure of activities

♦ Using the photocopiable master, explore with the children the variety of notes which are written in everyday life. Consider notes on telephone pads; notes in sketch form; notes under fridge magnets; notes on the doorstep or put through letter boxes; notes made from textbooks, radio or videos; cue prompts for videos and talks.

♦ The teacher models note-making as the writing of a main idea in brief, or in a succinct form. Discuss the beginning of Anthony Browne's *Piggy Book*. The mother's note to the family sums up the message of the first few pages of the book in three words – 'You are Pigs'. Do the children agree that this is the key point? What evidence can they find to support their opinion? The note and supporting evidence can be set out on paper:

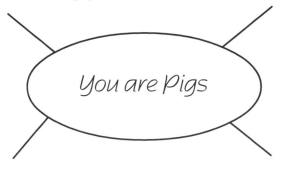

♦ Tell the children that they are going to make notes about a piece of text which will help them to draw a picture. Examples of texts which work well for this purpose include the description of *The Indian in the Cupboard* by Lynne Reid Banks, the description of Stig's cave in *Stig of the Dump* by Clive King, the description of Narnia as first seen by Lucy in *The Lion, the Witch and the Wardrobe* by C.S. Lewis or the description of Bilbo Baggins' home in *The Hobbit* by J.R.R. Tolkien. Let the children read the text, highlighting pieces which are useful as they go along. They can make up their own codes, eg green highlighter for nouns, yellow for adjectives, orange for phrases describing position/location. (See also the section on *Story Writing and IT*, page 48, for a related process.)

♦ Ask the children to make written notes, in the form of a table:

Object (s)	Description	Position/Location

♦ The children should now use their notes to draw a picture of eg the Indian, Stig's Dump or Narnia. Add labels and comment if desired. Check completed pictures against both the notes which were made in preparation for the task and the original text. How much agreement is there about the content of the pictures (key points)?

Extension

♦ Apply the same technique when asking children to work from passages describing characters, and draw pictures, eg Aunt Sponge and Aunt Spiker in *James and the Giant Peach* or the faun, Mr Tumnus, in *The Lion, the Witch and the Wardrobe*. Different table headings will be required.

♦ Re-present notes in another form, preferably one which requires concise writing, eg Lucy keeps a diary or sends a postcard from Narnia to the other children.

♦ Watch videos about authors. Record key words and summarise main ideas. Use the pause button.

♦ Look at fables and discuss the morals, the main ideas, contained within. Look at other examples of moral tales and ask the children to write down the key points and to list the supporting details.

♦ Take a chapter in a book and write it in note form.

♦ Re-present a picture book, or part of one, in note form.

♦ Write in note form a telephone message left on an answering machine.

♦ Summarise in note form the main idea of a paragraph from a non-fiction text.

♦ Discuss the fact that notes are not always in words. Making sketches and drawing symbols are valid ways of note-making.

Notes

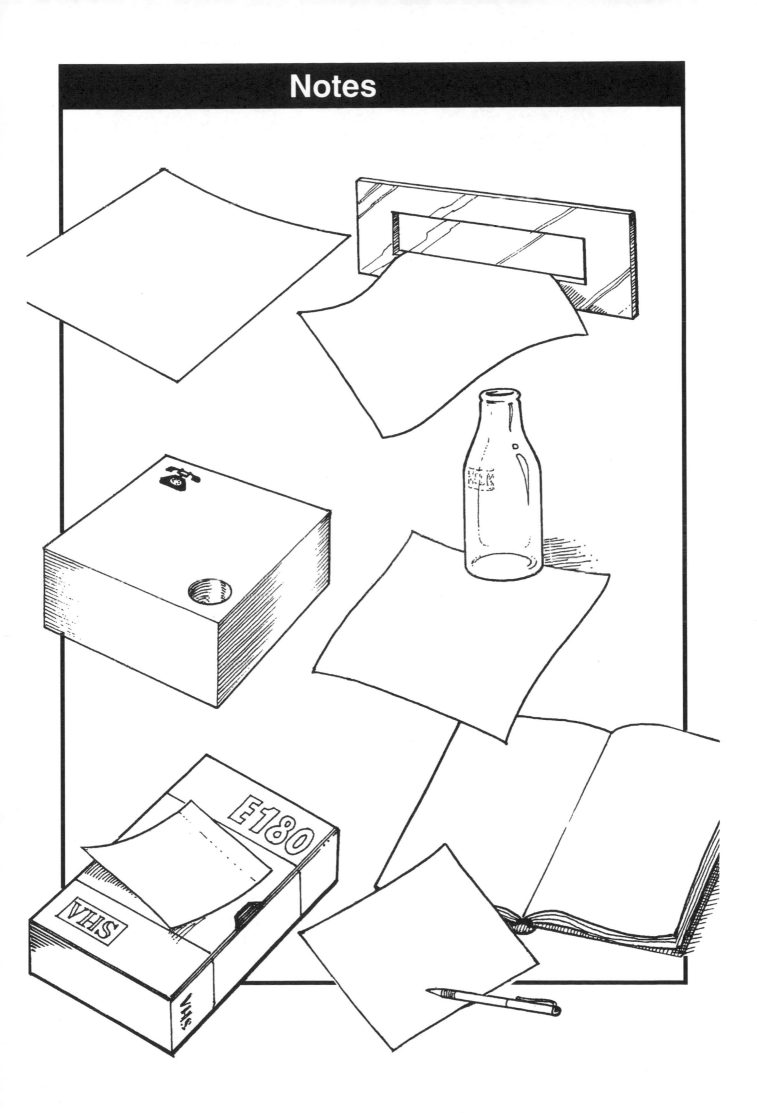

Stories

Many children enjoy writing stories when their imagination is stimulated. They often feel that what is needed to write better stories is simply to have better ideas, so focused work on story structure can help them to see that it is possible to enhance a simple story by structuring it well. This is one of the ways that children can learn to be aware of the audience for their stories, as they become conscious that they can make the tale more interesting for the reader by the way it is told.

Purpose

♦   to explore story structure, focusing on openings and endings

♦   to look at the strands of different plots in narrative writing

♦   to examine a story written by a child for the structure and plot

♦   to plan, draft and write a story.

Preparation and organisation

♦   Make a collection of story books which offer different openings. (The text models at the end of this activity offer some ideas.)

♦   Prepare copies of the photocopiable master on page 47 for children to work on in pairs or groups.

Timescale

♦   This unit of work may span one term.

Suggested sequence of activities

♦   Read the openings from a small number of books and discuss the effect each one has on the reader. Does it make you want to hear more? How much does it tell you? What can you guess from it? Discuss what kind of story the children think is contained in the books (eg traditional tale, modern adventure, science fiction, humorous). What are the clues that tell them this?

♦   The children can work in pairs to find three different openings from books in the book corner and share these with the whole group by reading them aloud. They could copy the first part of the different openings for other children to refer to (showing clearly the title, author and page number of the text they have chosen) and display this in the writing corner.

♦ Choose a story that everyone knows well. This could be a traditional tale or a book you have read aloud to the class recently. Talk about the structure of the story. What was the basic plot? Where did the 'complication' arise (ie where something interesting or unusual happened)? How did the author weave this into the story? Talk about the resolution of the story (ie how the situation was brought to a conclusion). Were they happy with the conclusion or did they find it disappointing? What were they expecting? Map the story structure together and discuss what would be the effect of taking out the complication.

♦ Read a short story to the class, stopping just before the resolution at the end. Ask the children to suggest how it might end and to explain how they came to their decision. Read the ending to the class and discuss how this is similar to or different from the suggestions made by the group.

♦ Talk to the group about the different endings they can remember from books they have read or that the whole class have heard. What makes story endings good or poor? Does the ending have to be a surprise? Can a good ending leave you wondering what happens next? What about stories with a message?

♦ Give out copies of the photocopiable master on page 47. This is a story written by a child of 11. Ask for the children's views. Talk about the opening and ask how the writer has made the reader want to know about the dangerous shell. Ask the children to trace the clues throughout the story that warn the reader that something was wrong, highlighting all the words or phrases that they find. Explain to the children that the writer has linked the incidents together so that each event leads on to the next.

♦ Ask them what they think of the character of Lisa. Would they like her as a friend? What clues tell them about her? What do they know about the character of the author? How do they know this? Make notes of the clues and what these tell the reader. Discuss the ending of the story. Do they like the ending? What do they think happens next?

♦ Working individually or in pairs, the children plan a story of their own paying particular attention to the opening, the plot, complication, resolution and ending. Stories can be drafted and revised for reading to the class or for display on the wall.

Extension

♦ With children working in small groups, use the game of *Consequences* to reinforce the features of a story. Each child writes a character's name on a piece of paper, folds over the writing and then passes the paper to the next child. This child suggests the personality of the character without looking at what has been written before. The paper continues round with the children adding another character, the setting of the story, how the action begins, the complication and resolution. These are read to the group and children use some of the ideas to plan a story of their own.

♦   For children who have a good grasp of story structure discuss with them the importance of *reflection* in their stories. Provide them with a well-known story and ask them to underline any text which is reflective. For example 'Red Riding Hood knew that she should stay on the path because ....' Then discuss with the group where further reflection could be inserted to improve the story. Finally ask the children to look at their own stories in draft to see if they have included any reflection. They could suggest further opportunities for reflection and see how this affects the story.

♦   Ask the children to do a metaphor hunt or simile hunt with a text like *Flither Pickers* by Theresa Tomlinson, *Jakey* from *Badger on a Barge* by Janni Howker or *Onion Tears* by Diana Kidd. Select from the list ones that could be included in a class collection of *Favourite Similes/Metaphors*.

♦   Write a glossary of dialect to accompany *Flither Pickers* by Theresa Tomlinson.

♦   See the work on openings in information writing in *Reports* section, page 56.

Text models

Openings

  Hansel and Gretel – Anthony Browne

  The Lion, the Witch and the Wardrobe – C.S. Lewis

  Fantastic Mr Fox – Roald Dahl

  Thunder and Lightnings – Jan Mark

  The Genie Trilogy – Anne Fine

Endings

  The Frog Prince Continued – Jon Scieszka

  Rent a Genius – Gillian Cross

  Bill's New Frock – Anne Fine

  It was a Dark and Stormy Night – Janet and Allan Ahlberg

  The Man Whose Mother Was a Pirate – Margaret Mahy

Plot

  Stories to Read Aloud compiled by Ian Souter – Scholastic

  Five Minute Stories – Scholastic. (These short stories contain some photocopiable material and are very useful for tracking plots, characters, openings and endings.)

Here is a story written by a girl of 11. It has been typed exactly as she wrote it.

An Unusual Shell

You wouldn't think a shell could be dangerous, would you? You wouldn't think a shell could be the difference between life and death, that a shell could stand you on a strange desert island would you? But I know different, I have been there – to that desert island, so these feelings I know.

The whole thing started in Lisa's house. Lisa, my ex-best friend. She collected things from all around the world. Strange things, unusual shells, elephants tusks, the feet of Rhino's. But she had one masterpiece, a massive, beautiful shell. She put a little of each of her things in there – a little powdered rhino horn, powdered gold, the bark of a palm tree, fractions of a hundred and one different oddities. I loved that shell. I loved picking it up, caressing it, holding it against my ear. I could hear the sands of the sea, of the wind rattling the trees.

I was holding it once when it was completely still and the sounds seemed clearer than ever... The sand between my toes? I opened my eyes and gasped in surprise. (Well wouldn't you) for I was standing on a beach, a beautiful beach – but it felt as if something was missing. Sometimes you can almost feel when some-one or something is angry, or happy, or surprised and I felt it now.

I couldn't work it out, as I began to pace the sands. The island was gorgeous. I could see the sparkling sea, the swaying palms trees, the mounds of glistening coral. But it was wrong. Everything felt wrong. I didn't even stop to think why I was there. What was I meant to be doing. It felt right that I should be there.

I sat down in the warm sand and closed my eyes. I could see Lisa having a tantrum about wanting more and I realised that we had seen everything differently. When I had seen a rhino racing across a great plain she had seen a nice piece of horn which could be made into jewellery or powdered. When I saw a tiger gracefully pouncing on its prey she had seen a cute little fur coat, perfect for winter. We even looked completely different. Her hair was coloured blonde and permed, her lips were always twisted into a spiteful pout. I had simple brown hair, and oh, this must be boring for you, but it's part of the tale. Everything fits. And that is when I realised, I suppose. Nothing should be taken from where it belongs. No-one should just be grabbed and taken away. Everything has the same right in this planet. A piece of shell should stay in its rightful place...

Just one thought, one wandering thought made me realise why I was on the island. I smiled at the shell I was still cradling in my arms, and laid it down on the sands. "Here" I whispered" This is where you belong." And with that, I walked towards the sea, knowing I had done what I had been put here for.

Discussion points

❋ How has the writer made us want to know more about the dangerous shell?

❋ What clues are there to warn the reader that something is wrong?

❋ What do you think of Lisa's character?

❋ What clues are there about the character of the author (the writer)?

❋ Do you like the ending?

Story Writing and IT

When information technology is integrated into teaching, it can open children's eyes to new ways of thinking about the structures and conventions of texts in a variety of media. Explicitly moving between 'living books' and conventional narrative can offer children the opportunity to explore and experiment with story in a way that will enrich their writing in general.

Purpose

♦ to explore and develop story structure using the genre of myth/folktale (classic and modern versions) with a CD-ROM

♦ to focus in depth on character development in narrative

♦ to develop the use of description to create atmosphere and imagery.

Preparation and organisation

♦ Class to explore and become familiar with the a 'Living Book' CD-ROM, in this case *Kiyeko and the Lost Night*, in pairs or small groups. Class discussion, reading of Classic Tales, and modelling lead to joint construction and deconstruction of children's own narrative writing.

♦ This approach can be taken with other CD-ROM Titles; *Broderbund Living Books* are of a reliable quality although some will be more appropriate than others.

Timescale

♦ This unit of work may span one term.

Suggested sequence of activities

♦ *Kiyeko* is used as a model for exploring story structure. First allow children, in small groups, to explore the story on screen. Then as a whole-class activity explore how the story is 'made up'. By asking a series of questions, help the children to recognise features of story narrative and particular features of this genre, eg Where does the story take place? How is the mood and atmosphere created? What moves the story on? What do the 'hot spots' (interactive areas of the screen where you click and something happens) add to the story? Make a list of everyone's ideas.

♦ Compare and contrast *Kiyeko* with a conventional narrative in a similar genre, eg the *Just So Stories* by Rudyard Kipling. Look for similarities, particularly the nature of endings.

♦ As a class activity, make story maps for *Kiyeko*. Refer to the list made earlier by the class. Maps should show the basic structure of the story.

♦ Using the story maps, build up a clear, explicit 'picture' of how this story is made. This activity can be differentiated. Discuss maps as a class.

♦ Returning to the screen, tell children that the purpose of the task is to produce a class book that tells the story of *Kiyeko* in conventional book form, not a screen version. Discuss the differences. Focus on those parts of the story on screen that need to be put into words to make the characters and events clear on paper, often passages of description or speech. Hot spots will need to be explained in words and will be structurally significant, ie the story moves on. The final purpose of the book may be to be placed in the book corner, sent to a software company or used with younger children in the school. A variety of audiences is possible.

♦ Children work in groups as before, this time with a focus on the main character Kiyeko. Using photocopies of selected speech from the modelled Kipling stories, let each group focus on speech for episodes where Kiyeko features on screen. Referring to the models, groups write speech for Kiyeko, adding to existing speech or replacing it. They must remember that the speech should tell the audience something about Kiyeko and/or move the story on. These could be displayed as speech bubbles.

♦ The groups continue to work on the same screen, rewriting the text for this screen using the newly collected speech and adding descriptive passages related to the hot spots. The teacher will need to input here with models and discussion of descriptive passages that create atmosphere and imagery, eg the opening scene of *The Iron Man* by Ted Hughes. One child in the group could act as scribe at the screen while the hot spots are used.

♦ Each group should now be ready to interweave both speech and descriptions to produce a much fuller text for each screen. Some of the refining and redrafting work can be done away from screen with collected notes and tabulations. Children will need to discuss what they are doing and consult with the teacher or other groups.

♦ Finally a team can bring the book together and edit it ready for publication, including illustration if desired. In a whole-class session, children can decide whether their telling of this tale is still typical of its genre or how it is different.

Extension

◆ Rewrite the story in a different voice (eg from the point of view of the snakes) or for a different audience.

◆ Work together on joint class or group construction of a similar text in the folktale genre, using a story planner and with a focus on character development or description.

◆ Make class guides to help write a myth. (The class could make these whenever a new genre is introduced.)

◆ Children collect their own 'bank' of examples (extracts) to be used as **models** for features of text types or genres.

eg *Diary* – Anne Frank	(atmosphere/imagery)
Tuck Everlasting – Natalie Babbitt	(atmosphere/imagery)
Trouble Half-Way – Jan Mark	(character development/dialogue)
Just So Stories – Rudyard Kipling	(myth/folktale genre)

CD-ROM models

There are many Living Book titles and the quality varies. The following are recommended:

Grandma and Me (Broderbund)

Tortoise and The Hare (Broderbund)

How the Leopard Got His Spots (Microsoft)

Kiyeko and the Lost Night (UBI Soft)

Brochures

Brochures provide children with examples of persuasive writing through publicity material. Directness, choice of tone, and the use of colourful language rich in adjectives and adverbs characterise much publicity material. Work on writing brochures will also involve children in paying close attention to accurate and relevant information and the ways in which it can be ordered and presented. Maps, symbols, bullet points, logos and other presentation features play a key role in making successful texts. The work can be tied in to school trips, work on local facilities, or guides to the school.

Purpose

♦ to consider the audience(s) for publicity materials through looking at examples

♦ to identify persuasive language (both implicit and explicit) by studying examples of publicity materials

♦ to recognise that the purpose of publicity material is to persuade as well as to inform

♦ to identify features of layout and presentation

♦ to present information persuasively in a brochure format.

Preparation and organisation

♦ Class collects examples of publicity materials, to include brochures and leaflets for tourist attractions. Depending on the age and ability of the class, it may be best to focus on brochures aimed at children. Preparatory work and discussion lead to individual or collaborative work to write a brochure. (The photocopiable master on page 54 can be used to support this work.)

Timescale

♦ This work may occupy two weeks.

Stages with teacher

◆ Discuss the examples of publicity materials collected by the children and yourself. What is their purpose? Who are the writers trying to persuade? What are they trying to persuade them to think and/or do? How are they attempting to do this? Will they be successful?

◆ Sort the materials into categories agreed by the group or class. Categories could include such aspects as audience, level of detail, adequacy of information, extent or quality of illustration, layout features, appeal to the group. Decisions about these aspects should be justified orally.

◆ Allow children to focus in groups or pairs on the language used, to provide guidelines for their own 'advertising agency'. Titles, openings, headings, and punchy final messages are good for closer study. Other features may be explored, eg rich use of adjectives, the use of intensifiers (*entirely* satisfied, *thoroughly* relaxed) to give the sense of a personal author, repeated use of *you* to make the reader feel personally involved and, by contrast, impersonal presentation of information to make it sound authoritative. These findings will need to be drawn together as a whole-class activity.

◆ Distribute the photocopiable sheet *Barminster-on-Sea*. Alternatively, draw on current reading or topic work to choose an appropriate location as the focus of the brochure – the school, the local neighbourhood, places visited on school trips. (It is important that children should not be asked to rewrite existing brochures: unless there is a definite change of purpose or audience, they will feel their efforts are overshadowed by glossy originals.)

◆ Discuss the purpose, audience and form for this piece of writing. In groups or pairs (or with the whole class) brainstorm ideas for titles, layout, details for inclusion, illustration, things that would persuade people to come to Barminster, appropriate language of persuasion. It may be helpful to impose some constraint on length or layout, eg the brochure must occupy no more than two sides of A4 paper.

◆ Using IT or more traditional methods, children then work on initial drafts and revisions, leading up to final production for display.

Extension

◆ Take one brochure. Search and keep a tally – How many phrases? How many commands? How many questions? Ask children for their observations. Would the tally be significantly different if they compared them with the tallies made for instructions?

◆ Blank out all adjectives/adverbs from a brochure. Ask children what difference that would make.

♦ Take a brochure or leaflet written for adults and rewrite it for children.

♦ Examine publicity leaflets or advertisements for a product or service (eg a car, Channel Tunnel). Pick out the similarities and differences in language and approach between this and the tourist leaflets.

♦ Write a publicity leaflet which uses words to make something unusual sound attractive, eg persuading people to keep snakes, 'for sale' advert for a ruined building, job advert for chimney sweeps.

Contact Tourist Information Centres for leaflets and guides relating to your area.

Museums and libraries are also likely to have useful information about local attractions.

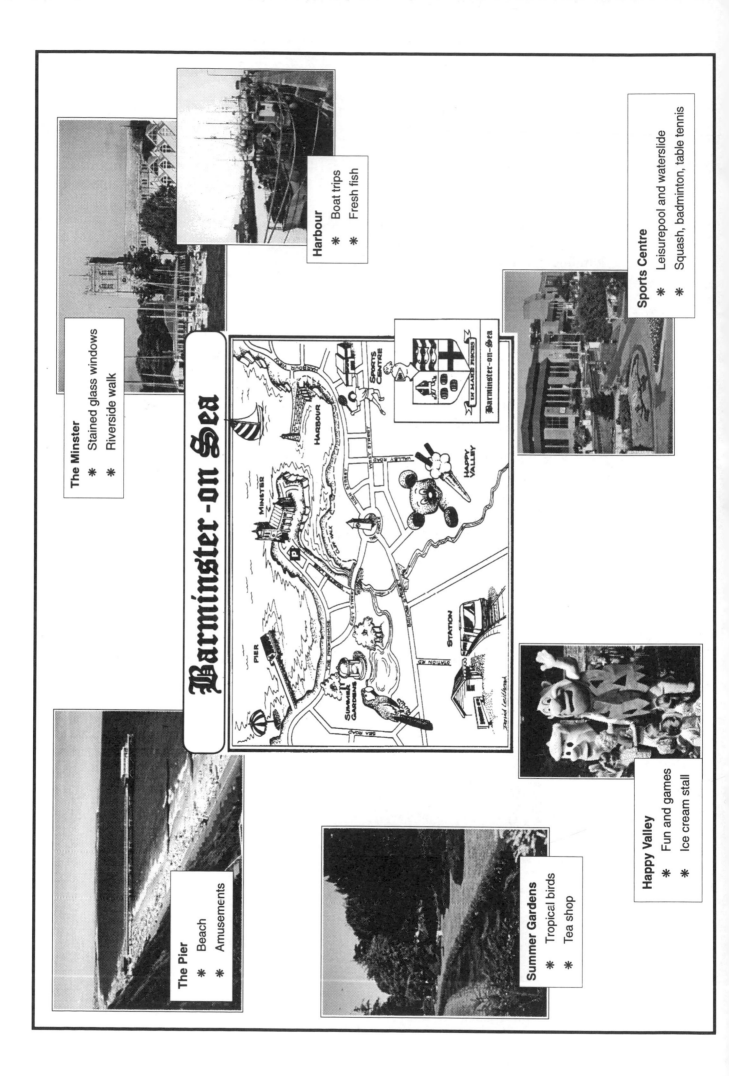

Barminster-on-Sea

The Minster
* Stained glass windows
* Riverside walk

Harbour
* Boat trips
* Fresh fish

Sports Centre
* Leisurepool and waterslide
* Squash, badminton, table tennis

The Pier
* Beach
* Amusements

Summer Gardens
* Tropical birds
* Tea shop

Happy Valley
* Fun and games
* Ice cream stall

Reports

Report writing is one of the types of information writing most frequently required of children in different curriculum areas. All too often, children will resort to copying chunks of information out of books, or give only one or two of the more noteworthy facts about a phenomenon they have been asked to write about. When children are supported in the writing of information texts such as these, however, they learn how to structure their work and how to use language effectively and appropriately.

Purpose

♦   to write a report for the peer group classifying and describing a natural phenomenon

♦   to make explicit the language and structural features associated with writing a factual report.

Preparation and organisation

♦   Reports can be approached as part of general topic work, or following a visit. The class will need access to information resources (which could include posters, reference books, videos, CD-ROM, an outside speaker) on the subject of the report. Children work in groups or pairs.

♦   The writing 'A Report on Barn Owls' on page 57 followed a visit to a school by an ornithologist. It provides an example of report writing and has been annotated to show assessment in practice.

Suggested sequence of activities

♦   Discuss the audience for the report (in this case the peer group). Discuss also the level of formality required. (This may be particularly relevant if the information has been presented by a speaker.)

♦   Discuss the information sources used, and brainstorm all the facts children can recall. (This can be done as a group or whole-class activity.)

♦   While listing the facts on a chart, talk about *defining terms* to clarify information and *expanding ideas* to elaborate the information given. Make a note of technical vocabulary (eg *nocturnal, satellite dish, carnivore*) and discuss its meaning.

♦ Introduce the idea of grouping information and using subheadings to organise it. Discuss appropriate subheadings based on the facts already listed (eg habitat, food) and explore whether important areas have been missed. An opportunity exists here and elsewhere in this topic to refer to work on *Making Notes* on page 40.

♦ Discuss the importance of an introductory statement, allowing children to work with a partner to compose a suitable introduction. Although their primary purpose will be to inform, they may also consider how to make their introduction interesting. (There are links here with work on story openings, on page 44.)

♦ Consider ways of organising the main points, bearing in mind the needs of the reader. Issues such as sequence, level of detail, and layout should be discussed here. At this point, children can divide into pairs or work individually on particular subheadings, referring back to the brainstorm charts.

♦ Review and revise completed drafts in the light of comments from others.

♦ Prepare to make final copy of texts for presentation as separate reports, 'fact boxes' on a chart, or individual fact cards.

A REPORT ON BARN OWLS
(Written by two children following joint work by their class)

LANGUAGE FEATURES

* constant use of subject referents

* uses simple present tense

* uses verbs for behaviour (*eats, fly, pick up*)

* subject and verb generally consistent with some exceptions; eg *The Barn Owl ... they*

* uses simple sentence structure, with connectives such as *because, so that*

Ways of describing

* uses adjectives and noun, eg *sharp claws, furry speckled feathers, endangered species*

* frequently uses very specific adjectives, eg **satellite dish**

* uses an appropriate simile, eg *face like a plate* (an older child might write *plate-like face*)

The Barn Owl
The Barn Owl is a bird of prey. It is an endangered species, it lives in barns and trees. They are nocturnal

Description
Its face is like a plate which is used as a satellite dish. The sound bounces off.

The feet
The Barn Owl has tiny feet and sharp claws because it has to pick up its prey.

The colour
It has brown speckles and a white face. It has white under the wings and a white belly. There are furry-speckled feathers on its back.

Habitat
The Barn Owl lives in barns and chimneys. The Barn Owl does not make nests.

Food
It is a carnivore and it eats mice, rats, wild gerbils and baby rabbits.

Movement/Speed
The Barn Owls fly fast and silent and glides and it flies low, so that the prey can't hear it coming. The Owl is endangered because people are moving to barns and also because mice eat chemicals and the owls eat the mice and they die.

PURPOSE AND ORGANISATION

* has a general classification

* has description grouped under subheadings

* includes physical and behavioural characteristics

* uses subheadings to define paragraphs

* each paragraph begins with a reference to the subject, eg '*The Barn Owls ...*', '*It ...*'

* uses explanation appropriately to conclude text

Poetry

Children often have a natural enjoyment of the economy and pattern of poetry. Teachers sometimes feel that studying poetry may dampen this enthusiasm, but there are ways of exploring poetry that are lively and interesting. Close attention to the purposes and patterns of poetry will help children to write more effectively themselves, as well as enhancing their appreciation of others' poems.

Purpose

♦   to develop an appreciation of different communicative purposes being realised in the form of poetry

♦   to develop awareness of the reader (audience)

♦   to explore structures and patterns of language and their effect in poetry

♦   to write poetry.

Approach

♦   Immersing the whole class in shared texts, moving on to discussion as a class and small groups, exploring texts, and collaborative or individual writing.

Timescale

♦   This work needs to take place over a period of time, eg half a term or a term.

Suggested sequence of activities

♦   Use an anthology such as *The Thirteen Secrets* by Adrian Mitchell and Valerie Littlewood, as a starting point. Explain to children the purpose of the activities.

♦   Read the complete book to the class for a poetry focus, reading from it every day for at least a week. Give children time to browse, reflect and read in pairs as well as independently over several weeks (**immersion**).

♦   Children then in pairs or groups select a favourite poem from the book and work on presenting or re-presenting the text to the class, eg tapes, drama or role play.

This leads to **familiarity** with the poems and recognition of the 'song and dance' in this form of writing. Discuss the children's presentations. Identify the different purposes of the poems, eg *There Will Come Soft Rains* is an expository/persuasive poem.

♦ Taking a favourite poem from the anthology, write it on a large board and lead children in brainstorming and sharing ideas about likes, dislikes, patterns, puzzles. Children and teacher can write comments to discover how the poem has been made, how and why it works (**exploration** of text). The activity may be repeated with another poem.

This approach can be called a Detective Game. Here are some issues you might discuss in relation to *Double Glazing* by Brian Patten.

What is the purpose of this poem? (Does it describe? Does it protest?) Is it happening now or another time? How does it make the reader feel? Who tells the poem? Focus on the language, eg

Patterns/repetition	*Jenny lives, She'll not say.*
Rhyme lines	2 and 4, at the end of the line.
Metaphor	*double-glazed.*
Play on words	*tough nut to crack.*

♦ Let the class write their own poetry 'secrets'. Choose a structure that the class feels comfortable with eg prose or four-line rhyming verse as in *The Thirteen Secrets*. Work in pairs using the photocopiable master on page 61. Display the finished poems. It is the secret itself that has priority here. (At this point you can assess how far children have begun to understand the way poems work.)

♦ Work on a joint class construction of a poem using as a model the poem already explored. Use a familiar subject matter, eg cross-curricular themes. Children contribute their ideas, and you act as guide and scribe. The photocopiable master on page 62 will provide a useful structure.

♦ Working in pairs, children can either select another poem from the anthology and use its structure and shape to act as a model for their own poem or they may choose a 'secret' and develop their own structure, shape and patternings for writing a poem. Refer children to the models: the text that was explored as a class, as well as the constructed class poem. Pool ideas and jottings and collections of phrases and words, encourage use of a thesaurus. This is where it may be necessary to provide some sort of framework (eg matrix, flow chart, headings) to help in the structuring of the poem (see photocopiable master). It is important to take several weeks at this stage, leaving the drafting then returning to work on it again. (There are possibilities for assessment here with regard to the drafting process.)

♦ The next stage is to shape these draft ideas into a poem format, again drafting, leaving work, and returning to the drafts. Encourage discussion with other children and adults. The final steps would be editing and publishing the poem (optional).

Extension

♦ Look at other anthologies, eg *Classic Poems to Read Aloud* selected by James Berry.

♦ Children make their own anthologies, using a specific text type or theme, of their own poems or poems collected from other writers.

♦ Children look at a particular text type (eg narrative within poetry) and find examples of these, such as *Hiawatha* (Longfellow), *Jesse James* (Thirteen Secrets), *The Owl and the Pussy Cat* (Lear). They then write their own poems using this text type.

♦ Children rework a poem from *The Thirteen Secrets* using a different text type/ voice.

♦ Take a published poem and blank out verbs or nouns. What do the children notice? Can they tell what the poem is about? Ask children 'What do those words have in common? What do they **do**?'

♦ Write a short poem of accumulated phrases which ends with a verb, eg The suitcase, By the sea, On the shingle in the moonlight, GROANED.

Text models

The Thirteen Secrets – Adrian Mitchell and Valeric Littlewood

Classic Poems to Read Aloud – selected by James Berry

The Kingfisher Book of Children's Poetry – ed. Michael Rosen

Sky in the Pie – Roger McGough

What Is the Truth – Ted Hughes

Come on in to My Tropical Garden – Grace Nichols

Song of the City – Gareth Owen

Earthways Earthwise – ed. Judith Nicholls

Poetry Secrets

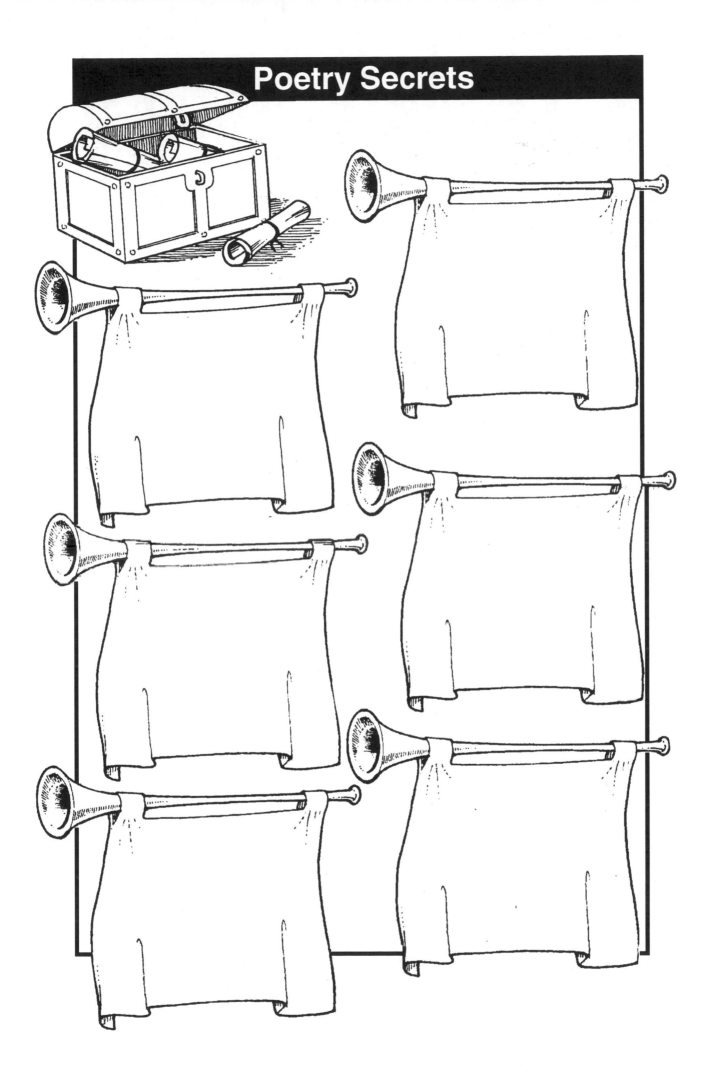

Poetic Reflections

Full rhyme

FONT SIZE and TYPE

Regular pattern AABB ; ABAB

adjectives

Repetition

Calligrams

Calm Serene

Onomatopoeia CRASH!

Half rhyme below – shadow

Cinquains 22 Syllables 2 4 6 8 2

Haiku 17 Syllables 5 7 5

Carefree humorous

Metaphor rooted to the spot

Line length

Sad gloom

Rap

Verses

Similes like... as...

Title ——————

Type of poem

Audience

Shape	Images	Mood/ Atmosphere	Rhythm	Reading the poem aloud eg tone; alone or with others; speed...

CHILD'S WORK

Tudor Spirit

Soul leaving modern day.
Entering old Tudor age.
Muddy water-logged roads.
Foul smells all around.
Pandemonium everywhere.
Pictures instead of writing.
Entering where my,
Prospective residence stands
Whiffs like rotting garbage.
Rats giving people plague.

Robbers plaguing folk nightly.
Tired at dawn.
Lying down thinking.
What if my soul stays?
So turning over.
Hearing radio blasting out.
Back home modern day.

By Timothy (Year 4)

Teacher's comments

use of present participle	*leaving, entering*
descriptive phrases	*like rotting garbage*
choice of vocabulary	*prospective, garbage, pandemonium*
alliteration	*people plague*
play on words	*plaguing folk nightly* and *giving people plague*
extended noun phrase	*Muddy water-logged roads*
use of hyphen	
line length to control reader pace and create atmosphere	*So turning over.*
patterns	Line length, few non-lexical words
repetition	*entering*
image	*Pictures instead of writing*

Timmy worked at this piece over a three-week period, drafting and redrafting several times. He enjoyed the making of the poem, especially playing with words, and is certainly beginning to feel how to write using metaphor and imagery. He was fascinated by the work with the thesaurus and we spent time discussing the appropriateness of words, subtle shades of meaning, and fitness for context. This is how the word *foul* was chosen.

Given the choice between taking home his drafts or a final copy of the poem, Timmy took the drafts.

ASSESSMENT

Assessing Writing

What principles underpin effective assessment practice?

Appropriate assessment helps to promote effective teaching and learning. By reviewing children's achievements and reflecting on their progress it is possible to identify specific needs, and to determine which learning opportunities will help children to move forward. This is essential to good curriculum planning. It is particularly helpful if reviews are carried out *with* individual children, as children's motivation and commitment can be increased when they are involved in a process of self-assessment, or where assessment is negotiated with the teacher. Negotiated assessment should always take account of and value children's social, cultural and language experiences, and the process is enhanced if parents can be involved in some way. All this has major implications for the way children's learning is assessed.

Here are some principles to consider when monitoring assessment in the classroom. Assessment should

- inform curriculum planning;

- be based on clear learning objectives;

- be integrated into classroom activities;

- be appropriate to the task;

- allow for unexpected as well as intended outcomes;

- draw on a wide range of evidence and learning experiences;

- place achievement in context;

- indicate strengths and identify areas for development;

- involve children in reflection and review;

- inform teachers and children about individual progress;

- focus on teaching processes as well as learning outcomes.

What features of classroom management and organisation support effective assessment in writing?

Assessment of children's writing is effective where learning is appropriately organised and children are given the opportunity to

- set and agree learning objectives;

- ♦ have access to a wide range of literature which exemplifies quality writing offered through a range of teaching styles;

- ♦ discuss with their teacher and other children their thoughts and plans so that they can express their thoughts and refine their thinking;

- ♦ learn in different ways and use their wide range of experiences to inform their writing;

- ♦ work collaboratively;

- ♦ write for a wide range of audiences, some of whom may respond and be interactive.

All of these principles of classroom management and organisation are reflected in the individual writing activities in the *Practical Activities* section of this book.

How do we plan for effective assessment of writing?

Teachers need to identify the type of activities that will provide children with a **range of writing experiences** so that an appropriate range of work can be assessed. This book can help ensure an appropriate range is covered. Each of the Practical Activities covers a different type of writing, and helps to identify the **learning opportunities** that children should be given as they experience the range of different types of writing.

Teachers also need to identify key learning objectives in their planning, and it is these objectives that help to provide the criteria for assessment. Each of the writing activities offered in this book, for example, starts with a statement of *purposes*, and these may be used to formulate **criteria for assessing work** – in other words, criteria for success – either as it progresses or when it is complete.

As well as tracking children's development and progress to date, information from assessments should in turn inform the experiences they will be offered in the future, and the *extension* activities included in the Practical Activities section of this book can be used to **plan learning opportunities** to support a child's development within a particular type (or genre) of writing.

How do we assess writing?

Teachers continually make assessments in a range of ways: observing children while they are working, listening to them as they discuss their work, marking work, reflecting on the work, and occasionally – perhaps once or twice a year – carrying out in-depth analysis of focused assessment tasks. *It is neither necessary nor desirable to keep a detailed written record of all these assessments.*

In order to come to a judgement about a child's writing, teachers will need to observe the *process* of writing (planning, drafting, revising) as well as the finished product.

These judgements can then be used to inform either formative or summative assessment processes.

The 1995 Orders for English can help schools and teachers to plan and make judgements about children's work. The revised Orders specify common requirements: programmes of study to guide planning and teaching; and attainment targets to guide summative judgements. Level descriptions now replace the old statements of attainment as the basis for making judgements about attainment. They indicate the typical characteristics of performance for children working at a particular level. Teachers should use their knowledge of children's work across a range of contexts to judge which level description best matches an individual child's attainment. Substantial and helpful guidance on making these judgements is given in the SCAA document *Consistency in Teacher Assessment: Exemplification of Standards* (SCAA, 1995).

Focused assessments for in-depth analysis

As well as making ongoing judgements about children's work, teachers will find it helpful to plan occasional focused assessment opportunities to enable judgements to be made about a particular aspect of writing. The Practical Activities in this book may prove useful for this purpose. Such detailed analysis takes time, and should be undertaken only occasionally. It might be carried out at the end of a unit of work, say, or in response to concerns about an individual child; or as an in-service activity to develop common understanding among staff about the assessment of writing within the school.

The assessment criteria for the 1995 key stage 2 English tests provided teachers with a particularly useful set of practical guidelines for assessing children's writing in depth. They enabled teachers to note the way children structure their work and make choices about language, as well as their developing use of punctuation. The assessment grids found on pages 72 to 80 of this book are based on this. These will be valuable not only for in-depth analysis of children's work, but also in informing less formal assessments carried out from day to day in the classroom, and in informing curriculum planning.

The appropriate place to specify the *detail* of a focused assessment would be in an individual teacher's short-term planning. Where a series of focused assessments are to be carried out across the school – across all key stage 2 classes, for example – language co-ordinators may wish to include *broad outlines* of each assessment in the school's medium-term planning. The Practical Activities in this book will help to identify the range of writing opportunities such a programme might include.

It is particularly helpful to keep a small selection of writing for each child which can be updated at regular intervals. These annotated pieces of writing should represent significant progress for the child and cover a range of the different types of writing done at this key stage.

Planning a writing task

When planning a writing task, plans should reflect individual needs as well as the particular aspects of writing that are to be assessed. Pupils should also be involved in setting targets for the work so that they will have clear criteria for success as they carry their learning forward.

When planning a focused assessment in writing it is helpful to consider at the outset:

- children's previous experience;
- the specific learning objectives;
- the processes involved in the type of writing proposed;
- how the task will be presented and any implications this will have for assessment.

Providing feedback on work

In responding to children's work teachers may provide feedback in a number of different ways. Feedback might include:

- responding appropriately to the content of what is written;
- recognising and praising children's achievement as the work proceeds;
- providing feedback on secretarial skills;
- editing aspects of work together;
- recognising achievement using an agreed marks scheme which is understood by pupils and parents;
- setting targets for the future.

Extending writing

In response to information from formative assessments teachers may wish to help children develop their writing in a particular genre. The following questions may help in planning future work:

- At what stage is the child's writing in relation to this particular type of text?
- How should the child's writing be taken forward?
- What should the child experience next?
- What learning opportunities need to be offered so that the child can develop his/her writing further?

The *extension* section in the Practical Activities could be useful in planning learning opportunities within a particular type of writing.

Summative assessment: providing information for reporting purposes

At the end of each year

Teachers may wish to summarise children's achievements at the end of the school year. This can be done by reviewing the judgements made about individual children as they worked across a range of contexts and judging which level description best describes their overall attainment. (Where practicable, children and parents could be involved in this review of progress.) A summary of the conclusions should be written in the annual report and school record.

At the end of the key stage

At the end of Year 6, teachers should use the information they have gathered on progress and attainment, based on the child's work in a range of contexts, in making a judgement for the statutory teacher assessment. Together with information from Years 3-5 where appropriate, it should be used in judging which level description best fits the child's overall attainment at the end of key stage 2.

ASSESSMENT GRIDS

THE DEVELOPMENT OF STORY WRITING

PURPOSE AND ORGANISATION	GRAMMAR	STYLE	SPELLING	HANDWRITING	END OF KS JUDGEMENT
• Attempts to write letters voluntarily. • Knows the difference between drawing/writing. • Writes from left to right and from top to bottom of page. • Attempts to write own first name. • Writes own first name correctly. • Uses some letters to represent words. • Can create own story orally, perhaps using toys or sequence of pictures. • Can retell a known story. • Can tell a story from their own experience. • Understands the spoken language can be written.	• Some word division.		• Writes some letter shapes in response to letter sounds/names. • Some identification of first and last letters.	• Experiments with a variety of writing materials. • Has effective pencil grip and control of writing tools. • Beginning to form letters correctly.	**Early development of writing.**
Writing communicates meaning through simple words and phrases. • One or two word observations. Often a mixture of observations and comment.	• Word division mostly accurate. • Shows an awareness of how full stops are used (*but not in their writing*).	• Some control of word order.	• Is able to spell some words recognisably.	Letters are usually clearly shaped and correctly orientated.	**Level 1** Consider L2

PURPOSE AND ORGANISATION	GRAMMAR	STYLE	SPELLING	HANDWRITING	END OF KS JUDGEMENT
Communicates meaning in narrative form, showing some awareness of the reader. Ideas developed in a sequence of sentences. • Rudiments of appropriate structure, e.g. beginning, middle. Assumption that reader knows context. Often a list-like series of events or observations. • An opening, more than one character (*person, animal or object*) and two or more events in sequence. • Often string of events with minimal development of setting, characters or story structure	• Some sentences demarcated by capital letters and full stops.	• Uses some words more interesting than *big, get, good*. • Some ideas in sentences using spoken language structure and simple undeveloped vocabulary. • Ideas linked by *and/so, then*. Vocabulary often non-specific (*make do, get, have, go, thing, someone, something*). • May include story language such as '*one day*', '*suddenly*', '*The end*'.	Simple monosyllabic words usually spelt correctly – (*cat, eat, dog, sun, thank, much, shop*). Inaccuracies are good phonetic guesses (*eg becos*).	Letters are accurately formed and consistent in size.	Consider L1 **Level 2** Consider L3
Story format is used and beginning to be adapted to different readers. Sequences of sentences extend ideas logically. • Writing relates to title. Some sensible relationship between points/episodes. • Details to add interest. Some detail in the description of setting or characters' feelings or motives. • A simple ending. • Beginning to revise and redraft in discussion with the teacher, other adults, or other children in the class, paying attention to meaning and clarity as well as checking for matters such as correct and consistent use of tenses and pronouns.	• Basic grammatical structure of sentences usually correct. • Punctuation to mark sentences – full-stops, capital letters and question marks – is used accurately.	Words chosen for variety and interest. • Beginning to shape writing through an increasing complexity of sentences, using connectives to indicate relation between ideas. • Simple noun phrases (*one sunny day, a red light*). • Simple adverbs (*quickly, soon*). • Connectives indicate, eg contrast, connection in time, explanation (*but, so also, because, etc.*).	• Spelling is usually accurate including common polysyllabic words (*after, open, teacher, holiday, window, jumped, arrived, before*).	Handwriting is joined and legible.	Consider L2 **Level 3** Consider L4

PURPOSE AND ORGANISATION	GRAMMAR	STYLE	SPELLING	HANDWRITING	END OF KS JUDGEMENT
Writing is lively and thoughtful. Ideas are often sustained and developed in interesting ways and organised appropriately for the purpose and the reader. • Appropriately paced and coherent writing. • Some use of appropriate conventions. • Awareness of reader. May begin to use paragraphing. • Events are logically related. • Length of story well judged with respect to pacing and detail. • Beginning, middle and ending suitably distinguished. • Some significant interaction between characters. • Comments on characters or events show awareness of reader • Paragraph divisions may separate beginning and/or end. • Can discuss the organisation of their own writing; can revise and redraft the writing as appropriate, independently, in the light of that discussion.	Writing grammatically complex sentences, extending meaning. Full stops, capital letters and question marks are used correctly. Some additional punctuation marks being used within the sentence. • Consistent use of main tenses and pronouns. Basic punctuation conventions accurate in at least half of instances. • Comma may separate elements of sentence or items in a list. Where relevant: • inverted commas (speech marks) clarify where speech begins and ends in at least half of instances; • question marks and/or exclamation marks used correctly in most instances.	Vocabulary choices are often adventurous and words are used for effect. • Greater use of written language structures and vocabulary to organise meaning, including use of subordinating connectives and expanded noun phrases. • Some structures different from spoken language (*It was Friday morning and Class 6 were looking forward to their trip...*) • Well chosen vocabulary. • Connectives given order and emphasis (*if, when, rather than, although, so as to, as though*). • Some expansion before or after the noun (*a shiny blue machine, a large copper kettle*).	• Spelling is generally accurate including polysyllabic words that conform to regular patterns, (eg *underground, message, could, famous, right*).	Handwriting is fluent, joined and legible.	Consider L3 Level 4 Consider L5

PURPOSE AND ORGANISATION	GRAMMAR	STYLE	SPELLING	HANDWRITING	END OF KS JUDGEMENT
Writing is varied and interesting, conveying meaning clearly for different readers. • Well structured writing with convincing opening, central content and ending. Paragraphs mark main divisions. • Secure grasp of chosen narrative style or story type (eg *realistic narrative, fable, myth, adventure, etc.*). • Flexible use of narrative (eg *ability to experiment with story opening – starting in the midst of circumstances or with snatches of dialogue or with narrator's synopsis*). • Ending relates convincingly to central plot. • Interweaves elements of dialogue, action, description. • Development of point of view and 'narrative voice' (eg *asides to reader, comments on action, indication of character's thought and/or feelings*). • May attempt to develop more than one plot or line of narration (eg *via 'time-slip', or parallel stories*). • Can assemble ideas on paper or on a VDU, individually or in discussion with others, and show evidence of an ability to produce a draft from them and then revise and redraft as necessary.	Simple and complex sentences are organised into paragraphs. A range of punctuation, including commas, apostrophes and inverted commas is usually used accurately. Punctuation conventions generally accurate. Comma marks clauses or items in a list. Where relevant: • speech marks correct including comma to introduce/conclude direct speech • voices in dialogue clearly distinguished • appropriate use of question marks and/or exclamation marks.	Vocabulary choices are imaginative and words are used precisely. Appropriate use of Standard English. A variety of sentence constructions and vocabulary to clarify and emphasise meaning. • Appropriate choices between Standard English and slang, colloquialism or dialect shown in distinction between direct speech and narrative. • Writing distinguished from speech, eg passive voice to alter focus of attention (*I was surrounded by guards*); grouping subjects before a main verb or referring back/ forward to avoid repetition (eg *by using that, these, it*). • Varied and appropriate vocabulary. • Pace managed through varied sentence length.	Words with complex regular patterns are usually spelt correctly (*although, beautiful, delicious, straight, weights, furniture*).	Handwriting is joined, clear and fluent and where appropriate adapted to a range of tasks.	Consider L4 **Level 5** Consider L6

PURPOSE AND ORGANISATION	GRAMMAR	STYLE	SPELLING	HANDWRITING	END OF KS JUDGEMENT
Writing engages and sustains the readers' interest, showing some adaptation of style and register to different forms. • Beginning to adapt role of writer with confidence. • Detail and sequence competently managed to keep the readers' interest. • Use of paragraphs to support coherent organisation. • Cues the reader in with enough information to set the scene in the opening sentences. • Secure use of all conventions. • Development of theme (controlling ideas) as well as plot (the controlling of events). • A number of linked episodes. • Uses narrative devices such as reflection on characters and actions, non-linear time line, management of surprise. • Relationship/conflict between characters. • Can recognise when redrafting and revising are appropriate and act accordingly, either on paper or on a computer screen. • Demonstrates an increased awareness that a first draft may be changed, amended and reordered in a variety of ways. • Can show in discussion and in writing an awareness of what is appropriate and inappropriate language use in written texts.	Range of punctuation correctly used to clarify meaning. Ideas are organised into paragraphs. • Sustained accurate punctuation, with evidence of variation in clause and sentence length to assist reader. • Commas to avoid ambiguity in relating element of sentences. • Brackets or dashes introduce explanations or examples.	Pupils use a range of sentence structures and varied vocabulary to create effects. • Precise and varied use of language, chosen and organised for effect. • Varied choice of verbs (clambered, plodded) and adverbs (reasonably well behaved children) gives shades of meaning. • Alteration of word order for effect, eg to develop themes and sustain reader interest (All eyes were on the kangaroo, leaping effortlessly over the wild hedges). • Deliberate patterning for emphasis and rhythm (thunder sounded, lightning flashed, and the rain began to pour). • Characterisation through dialect, slang or colloquialism, as needed. • May use a simile or metaphor (The jeep was lurching like a wild thing).	Spelling is generally accurate, including that of irregular words.	Handwriting is neat and legible.	Consider L5 Level 6

THE DEVELOPMENT OF INFORMATION WRITING

PURPOSE AND ORGANISATION	GRAMMAR	STYLE	SPELLING	HANDWRITING	END OF KS JUDGEMENT
• Attempts to write letters voluntarily. • Knows the difference between drawing/writing. • Writes from left to right and from top to bottom of page. • Attempts to write own first name. • Writes own first name correctly. • Uses some letters to represent words.	• Some word division. • A mixture of letters/letter strings and words.		• Writes some letter shapes in response to letter sounds/names. • Some identification of first and last letters.	• Experiments with a variety of writing materials. • Has effective pencil grip and control of writing tools. • Beginning to form letters correctly.	**Early development of writing.**
• Meaning communicated through use of simple words and phrases or rudimentary statements, eg labelled diagram, picture captions. • Writing is made up of isolated statements. • Observations or points made are related to personal experience. • Little or no awareness of a reader.	• Word division mostly accurate. • Some punctuation may be evident.	• Some control of word order or structure, eg layout for instructions.	• Is able to spell some words recognisably.	• Letters are usually clearly shaped and correctly orientated.	Consider early stage **Level 1** Consider L2

PURPOSE AND ORGANISATION	GRAMMAR	STYLE	SPELLING	HANDWRITING	END OF KS JUDGEMENT
• The writing communicates meaning through a series of statements. • Individual points may be elaborated (though these may not be connected). • Rudimentary features of chosen form may be evident, eg opening statement, subheading.	• Some sentences demarcated by capital letters and full stops.	• Generally uses spoken language structures. • Undeveloped vocabulary with repetition. • Personal rather than impersonal voice used. • Vocabulary often non-specific. • Beginning to use some technical language, eg *wings, sharp claws*.	• Simple monosyllabic words usually spelt correctly – (*car, cat, dog, sun, thank, much, shop*). Inaccuracies are good phonetic guesses (eg *becos*).	• Letters are accurately formed and consistent in size.	Consider L1 **Level 2** Consider L3
• Basic feature of chosen text type evident, eg introduction, introductory statement; subheadings; tables/diagrams may be included; series of points and observations related to the topic. • Points may be clarified or elaborated, (eg *an extended piece of information*), explanation of an event, an expression of opinion. • Revisions and redrafts show evidence of attention to clarity of meaning and the needs of a reader.	• Basic grammatical structure of sentences usually correct (eg *main subject and verb agree*). • Full stops, capital letters and question marks used accurately.	• The beginnings of a written style are evident. • Connectives used to structure the writing and to provide links or contrasts, eg *sometimes, first, because, though*. • Verb tenses used appropriately.	• Spelling is usually accurate including common polysyllabic words (*after, open, teacher, holiday, window, jumped, arrived, before*).	• Handwriting is joined and legible.	Consider L2 **Level 3** Consider L4

PURPOSE AND ORGANISATION	GRAMMAR	STYLE	SPELLING	HANDWRITING	END OF KS JUDGEMENT
• Writing is thoughtful. Ideas sustained and developed and organised appropriately for the purpose and the reader. • Appropriately paced and coherent writing. • Awareness of reader evident, eg *expanded pieces of information*; detail beyond the simple; explanation and/or reason evident. • Paragraphs/subheadings may be used. • Revisions and redrafts show awareness of need to expand or reduce content. • Some concluding statement or summary is evident.	• The majority of sentences are correctly demarcated. • Within sentences there is some evidence of correct use of commas to separate elements of sentence: clauses, short phrases, items in a list.	• Meaning elaborated through use of complex sentences. • Greater use of written language structures and vocabulary to organise meaning including use of subordinate clauses, passive voice, expanded noun, phrases. • Words and phrases well chosen for interest or precision.	• Spelling is generally accurate including polysyllabic words that conform to regular patterns, (eg *underground, message, could, famous, right*).	• Handwriting is fluent, joined and legible.	Consider L3 **Level 4** Consider L5
• Well structured writing showing a secure grasp of chosen text (eg *information, description, discussion*). • Awareness of reader evident, (eg *detailed information*); development of a point of view; consideration of alternative viewpoints. • Confident use of paragraphs to organise either information or argument. • Revisions and redrafting show clarity of expression and evidence of awareness of reader. • Ideas are sustained and developed in an interesting way.	• Simple and complex sentences organised into paragraphs. • A range of punctuation, including commas and apostrophes used successfully. Where relevant: • writing may be organised into bulleted points; • a list or summary of points may be used; • brackets or dashes may be used.	• Style is both appropriate and confident. • Language used with precision and, where appropriate, imagination. • Standard English used throughout. • Varied and appropriate vocabulary. • Linguistic features such as passive and modal verbs (*should, may*) are used to effect eg *elephants should not be killed*.	• Words with complex regular patterns are usually spelt correctly (*although, beautiful, delicious, straight, weighs, furniture*).	• Handwriting is joined, clear and fluent and where appropriate adapted to a range of tasks.	Consider L4 **Level 5** Consider L6

PURPOSE AND ORGANISATION	GRAMMAR	STYLE	SPELLING	HANDWRITING	END OF KS JUDGEMENT
• Writing engages and sustains the reader's interest. • Reader alerted to the purpose of the writing. • Coherent organisation may include an introduction which establishes voice and tone. • A series of interlinked points or paragraphs. • A concluding statement or paragraph which is an appropriate summary, eg *either factual or persuasive.* • Revisions and redrafting show increased awareness of criteria for changes and amendments. • A sense of appropriate and inappropriate language to use in written texts.	• Range of punctuation used correctly to clarify/emphasise points. Ideas are organised into paragraphs. • Evidence of variation in clause and sentence length. • Commas are used to avoid ambiguity in relative clauses. • Colons or dashes used to introduce lists, explanations or examples.	• Sentence structure and vocabulary are used to create appropriate effects. • Chosen level of formality, tone, etc. is sustained throughout. • An impersonal style may be used, eg *it is well known.* • Word order may be altered for effect, eg *elephants, defenceless against guns, are ruthlessly slaughtered.* • Vocabulary is precise, varied and provides shades of meaning. • Simile or metaphor may be used.	• Spelling is generally accurate including that of irregular words.	• Handwriting is neat and legible.	Consider L5 Level 6

WRITING ASSESSMENT RECORD

WRITING ASSESSMENT RECORD

TASK

What type and form of writing has been asked for?

eg *recount, explanation, story, instruction; letter, diary, chart, poem*

CONTEXT

- nature of teacher input

- collaborative, group, individual

- degree of teacher intervention/support

- was the writer aware of any assessment focus?

STAGE OF WRITING

Draft – initial or revised

Final

(The analysis below is dependent on the stage of writing. At the plan/draft stage, assessment will be concerned with organisation of content; revision will focus on the writer's ability to reshape and rephrase for greater effect; the final piece of work on the coherence and impact of the whole, plus secretarial skills and layout.)

ANALYSIS

Purpose and organisation

(Range, Key Skills, Standard English and Language Study)
see *Assessment Grids*

Grammar and style

(Standard English and Language Study)
see *Assessment Grids*

Spelling, handwriting/presentation

(Key Skills)
see *Assessment Grids*

ADDITIONAL COMMENTS

WHERE NEXT FOR THE CHILD?

Experiences/teaching required for development

P.A.G.E. 1995

WRITING ASSESSMENT RECORD

NAME .... CLASS .... DATE ....

TASK

CONTEXT

STAGE OF WRITING

ANALYSIS
   Purpose and organisation

   Grammar and style

   Spelling, handwriting/presentation

ADDITIONAL COMMENTS

WHERE NEXT FOR THE CHILD?

P.A.G.E. 1995

BOOKLIST

AHLBERG, Allan   *The Jolly Christmas Postman*   London: Heinemann, 1991. 0-434-92532-2

AHLBERG, Allan   *The Jolly Postman : Or Other People's Letters*   London: Heinemann, 1986.   0-434-92515-2

AHLBERG, Janet and Allan   *It Was a Dark and Stormy Night*   London: Viking Children's Books, 1993.   0-670-84620-1

ATKINSON, Rowan and DRISCOLL, Robin   *Mr. Bean's Diary*   London: Boxtree,1993. 1-85283-349-1

BAKER, Jeannie   *Window*   London: Red Fox, 1993.   0-09-918211-4

BABBITT, Natalie   *Tuck Everlasting*   New York: Farrar, Straus and Giroux, 1988. 0-374-48009-5

BERRY, James (ed.) *Classic Poems to Read Aloud*   London: Kingfisher Books, 1995. 1-85697-253-4

BROWNE, Anthony   *Hansel and Gretel*   London: Walker, 1995.   0-7445-4364-9

BROWNE, Anthony   *Piggy Book*   London: Little Mammoth, 1989.   0-7497-0134-X

CROSS, Gillian   *Rent a Genius*   Harmondsworth: Penguin, 1993.   0-14-036130-8

DAHL, Roald   *Dirty Beasts*   Harmondsworth: Penguin, 1986.   0-14-050435-4

DAHL, Roald   *Fantastic Mr Fox*   London: Viking Children's Books, 1996.   0-670-85250-3

DAHL, Roald   *James and the Giant Peach*   Harmondsworth: Puffin Books, 1995. 0-14-037156-7

DARWIN, Charles   *Voyage of the 'Beagle'*   Harmondsworth: Penguin, 1989.   0-14-043268-X

EDWARDS, Viv   *Write Away*   London: Black, 1991.   0-7136-3468-5

FINE, Anne   *The Genie Trilogy*   London: Mammoth, 1992.   0-7497-1312-7

FINE, Anne   *Pack of Liars*   Harmondsworth: Puffin Books, 1990.   0-14-032954-4

FINE, Anne   *Bill's New Frock*   London: Methuen Children's Books, 1989.   0-416-12152-7

FRANK, Anne *Diary of Anne Frank* London: Pan Macmillian, 1995. 0-330-34188-X

HOWARTH, Lesley *Maphead* London: Walker Books, 1995. 0-7445-3647-2

HOWKER, Janni *Badger on a Barge* London: Walker Books, 1996. 0-7445-4352-5

HUGHES, Ted *The Iron Man: A Story in Five Nights* London: Faber, 1989. 0-571-14149-8

HUGHES, Ted *What is the Truth?* volume 2 of *Collected Animal Poems* London: Faber, 1995. 0-571-17624-0

IMPEY, Rose and PORTER, Sue *Letter to Father Christmas* London: Orchard Books, 1993. 1-85213-568-9

JAMES, Simon *Dear Greenpeace* London: Walker Books, 1993. 0-7445-3060-1

KEMP, Gene *The Turbulent Term of Tyke Tyler* London: Collins, 1984. 0-00-330021-8

KIDD, Diana *Onion Tears* Harmondsworth: Puffin Books, 1994. 0-14-034735-6

KING, Clive *Stig of the Dump* Harmondsworth: Puffin, 1993. 0-14-036450-1

KIPLING, Rudyard *Just So Stories* Harmondsworth: Puffin Books, 1994. 0-14-036702-0

LATHAM, Robert and MATHEWS, William (eds.) *The Shorter Pepys* Harmondsworth: Penguin, 1987. 0-14-043376-7

LEWIS, C.S. *The Lion, the Witch and the Wardrobe* London: Harper-Collins, 1994. 0-00-193977-7

MARK, Jan *The Dead Letter Box* Harmondsworth: Young Puffin Books, 1983. 0-14-031619-1

MARK, Jan *The One That Got Away* Aylesbury: Ginn, 1994. 0-602-25982-7

MARK, Jan *Thunder and Lightnings* Harmondsworth: Puffin, 1995. 0-14-036617-2

MARK, Jan *Trouble Half-Way* London: Viking Kestrel, 1985. 0-670-80188-7

McGOUGH, Roger *Sky in the Pie* Harmondsworth: Puffin, 1985. 0-14-031612-4

MAHY, Margaret *The Man Whose Mother Was a Pirate* Harmondsworth: Puffin Books, 1994. 0-14-055430-0

MITCHELL, Adrian and LITTLEWOOD, Valerie *The Thirteen Secrets of Poetry* Hove: Simon and Schuster Young Books, 1993. 0-7500-1379-6

NICHOLLS, Judith *Earthways Earthwise* Oxford: Oxford Paperback, 1993. 0-19-272248-4

OAKLEY, Graham *Diary of a Church Mouse* London: Macmillian Children's Books. 0-333-42614-2

OWEN, Gareth *Salford Road and Other Poems* Glasgow: Collins' Young Lions, 1988. 0-00-672919-3

OWEN, Gareth *Song of the City* London: Collins, 1987. 0-00-184846-1

PEARCE, Philippa *Tom's Midnight Garden* Harmondsworth: Puffin Books, 1993. 0-14-036454-4

REID BANKS, Lynne *The Indian in the Cupboard* London: Orion Children's Books, 1995. 1-85881-199-6

ROSEN, Michael (ed) *The Kingfisher Book of Children's Poetry* London: Kingfisher Books, 1991. 0-86272-784-7

SCIESZKA, Jon *The Frog Prince Continued* Harmondsworth: Puffin, 1992. 0-14-054285-X

SELWAY, Martina *Don't Forget to Write* London: Hutchinson, 1991. 0-09-176384-3

SELWAY, Martina *I Hate Roland Roberts* London: Red Fox, 1995. 0-09-918691-8

SOUTER, Ian *Stories to Read Aloud* Leamington Spa: Scholastic, 1993. 0-590-53847-X

TOLKEIN, J.R.R. *The Hobbit* London: Collins Educational, 1993. 0-00-330090-0

TOMLINSON, Theresa *Flither Pickers* London: Walker Books, 1992. 0-7445-2043-6

TOWNSON, Hazel *Deathwood Letters* London: Red Fox, 1991. 0-09-983500-2

WILSON, Jacqueline *Cliffhanger* London: Yearling, 1995. 0-440-86338-4

WILSON, Jacqueline *The Story of Tracy Beaker* London: Yearling, 1992. 0-440-86279-5

WAUGH, Sylvia *The Mennyms* London: Red Fox, 1994. 0-09-930167-9